Dr. Barbara

The Castor Oil Bible

The Complete Collection of
Barbara O'Neill's
Science-Backed Healing,
Beauty, and Holistic Wellness
Proven Remedies

Patricia Johnson

Table of Contents

STAY CONNECTED AND SHARE YOUR EXPERIENCES.

If you've enjoyed this book, make sure to visit my website for more information on holistic wellbeing and natural remedies. You'll find more tips, tools, and information about my other publications.

Your feedback is extremely important to me, and if you have the time, providing a review would be very appreciated.

Feel free to send images or even a video of how these cures worked for you; it benefits others and positively impacts our wellness community.

Thank you for taking part in this journey.

Scan The QR Code to visit my website

WWW.GYMEAVERSE.COM

Preface

As a health enthusiast with a preference for natural medicines, I've always been looking for holistic methods to improve my well-being. Castor oil came into my life when I discovered Barbara O'Neill's teachings . At the time, I was dealing with severe digestive troubles and chronic exhaustion, and I was becoming increasingly dissatisfied with conventional medical therapies that appeared to provide only temporary relief.

Intrigued by its reputation as a versatile medicine with a lengthy history of use, I wanted to learn more about castor oil's possible advantages. What I discovered was a fascinating world of ancient medicine that has been mostly ignored in modern treatment.

I began by adding castor oil to my regular routine. Initially, I applied it topically to relieve a reoccurring skin irritation. The results were amazing. Within a few days, the redness and irritation had faded, leaving my skin supple and healthy.

Inspired by these early accomplishments, I decided to look into the interior benefits of castor oil. I began by using it as a light laxative to treat my digestive difficulties. To my surprise, it brought alleviation that I hadn't received from earlier treatments. My problems decreased substantially, and I felt more energized.

As I continued to use castor oil, I became more conscious of its ability to promote overall health. I started experimenting with different applications, like applying it as a hair mask to boost growth and eliminate frizz. I also noticed that it can relieve muscle pain and tension when used in warm compresses.

My own journey with castor oil has been amazing so far; It has not only assisted me in addressing specific health difficulties, but has also encouraged me to pursue a more natural and holistic approach to healthcare.

I believe that castor oil is a wonderful tool for people of all ages and backgrounds, and through this book, I aim to share my knowledge and experiences with others, encouraging them to explore the incredible potential of this ancient treatment.

Introduction

In today's fast-paced world, when various health, beauty, and well-being solutions are marketed as quick fixes, many of us are taking a step back to analyze the goods we use and the impact they have on our bodies and the environment.
Synthetic chemicals, previously celebrated as breakthroughs, are now being studied for their long-term health implications, prompting many individuals to seek out more natural, holistic options. Castor oil has regained popularity as a result of the shift toward natural therapies.

At first look, castor oil may appear to be just another natural health supplement. However, castor oil is far from a momentary fad. It has been used for thousands of years and has survived due to its incredible versatility and efficacy.

Dr. Barbara Castor Oil Bible was intended to reintroduce you to this simple oil by providing a detailed, practical, and science-backed guidance on how to include castor oil into your health and beauty routine.

Still, this book is about much more than oil. It is about encouraging you to take charge of your health in a natural and sustainable manner. It's about simplifying wellness by offering you the tools you need to care for your body, skin, hair, and even your internal health with a single, all-natural product that has survived the test of time.

Why Castor Oil?

As you begin this journey, you may wonder: why castor oil? Why does this particular oil require a whole book? The answer is broad as demonstrated not just by its long history of use, but also by scientific studies that confirms its efficacy today.

Castor oil is unique among natural oils because it includes ricinoleic acid, a rare and strong molecule that contributes to many of its extraordinary qualities. Castor oil goes above and beyond what other oils do to nourish and soothe. It penetrates deeply and works at the cellular level to hydrate, heal, and repair.

This makes it one of the most versatile oils available, capable of treating a wide range of conditions, including skin irritation, digestive health, hair care, and joint discomfort.

This book will teach you that castor oil is both an efficient skin treatment and a potent inside medicine. It can be utilized to boost the body's natural healing processes, allowing you to manage pain, inflammation, and even detoxify your body.

This is more than just surface-level beauty, but it does play an important part. It is about taking a holistic approach to wellness, recognizing the body as an integrated system where beauty and health emanate from within.

Castor oil also has practical applications in the home. As more and more people are searching for environmentally friendly alternatives to chemical-laden cleaning solutions, castor oil offers a safe, natural answer for home care.

The Purpose of This Book: A Guide for Natural Wellness.

The intent of *Dr.Barbara Castor Oil Bible* is to provide a complete reference that will demystify castor oil and show you how you can use it effectively for your particular needs. Many people are familiar with castor oil, but they may not completely understand its uses or how to incorporate it into their daily routines.

This book seeks to fill that gap by providing clear, practical guidelines based on scientific research and centuries of traditional practice.

You may have come here because you're fed up with over-the-counter products that promise enormous effects but frequently fall short.

You may be looking for a solution to streamline your self-care routine while still addressing important issues such as aging skin, thinning hair, or digestive problems. Maybe you want to reduce your dependency on pharmaceuticals for chronic pain or inflammation.
Whatever your motivation for researching castor oil, this book is intended to meet you where you are and introduce you to better, more natural answers.

Its goal is about giving you the information and confidence to manage your health in an effective and sustainable manner. You don't need a cabinet full of products when a single, time-tested oil can solve so many of your problems.

As you progress through the chapters, you will get a better understanding of castor oil's qualities and how they perform in various applications. You'll understand not only the "what" but also the "why" of each application, making it easier for you to fit the oil to your individual requirements.

Here's an overview of what you can expect to learn:

Science of Castor Oil

One of the first themes we'll examine is the science behind the use of castor oil. We'll look at the oil's molecular composition, specifically its high content of ricinoleic acid, and explain how this component interacts with the body to provide its numerous advantages. Understanding the science is critical because it allows you to get beyond anecdotal evidence and be sure that castor oil is a valid, effective treatment for a wide range of problems.

Castor oil is more than just a classic home medicine, with anti-inflammatory characteristics and the ability to penetrate deep into the skin and stimulate cellular repair. It is a scientifically validated, multi-purpose treatment that has been demonstrated to be useful for a variety of health issues.

Pain Relief and Joint Health: Natural Solutions for Inflammation and Arthritis

One of the most important applications of castor oil is its ability to relieve pain and inflammation, especially in people suffering from arthritis or chronic muscle discomfort. Castor oil has been used for generations as a natural therapy for various problems, and contemporary science confirms its efficacy.
This book will teach you how to utilize castor oil packs to alleviate joint pain and inflammation.
- The science behind castor oil's anti-inflammatory characteristics and why it works so well for illnesses such as arthritis.
- Safe and effective ways to use castor oil into your pain management regimen, either as a stand-alone treatment or in combination with other therapies.

For anyone wishing to lessen their dependency on over-the-counter pain treatments or prescription pharmaceuticals, this section provides practical, science-backed options that are simple to include into your daily routine.

Internal Health: Aiding Digestion and Detoxification

While castor oil is most frequently associated with external applications, it also has great internal benefits. For thousands of years, castor oil has been used as a natural laxative and detoxifier. However, castor oil must be used internally with caution and accuracy.

This section explains how to use castor oil safely to improve digestion and treat constipation.
- The function of castor oil in cleansing the body and maintaining liver health.
- How to incorporate castor oil into your health routine without abusing it, ensuring that you get the advantages while avoiding unwanted side effects.

This section discusses a deliberate and balanced approach to utilizing castor oil internally, prioritizing safety and moderation. You'll leave with a solid understanding of how castor oil can benefit your overall digestive health and contribute to a more balanced, detoxified body.

Castor Oil in Skincare: The Secret to Radiant and Youthful Skin

Skincare is one of the most common use for castor oil, and with good reason. Castor oil has a unique capacity to moisturize and nourishing the skin, making it great for treating dry skin, minimizing fine lines and wrinkles, and creating a more youthful skin.

This section explains how to use castor oil for daily skin hydration.
- Castor oil-based face mask recipes for wrinkle reduction, skin tone evenness, and collagen synthesis.
- Treatment solutions for common skin disorders including acne, eczema, and psoriasis, with an emphasis on natural, compassionate healing.

You'll discover why castor oil is so beneficial to skin health and how it compares to other popular oils and treatments on the market. By the end of this part, you'll be able to construct your own specific skincare routine with castor oil as its foundation.

Castor Oil for Hair Health: Strengthening and Revitalizing at the Roots

If you've ever had thinning hair, a dry scalp, or dull hair, you're not alone. Many people experience these concerns as they age, and while there are numerous products available, few provide the natural, long-term benefits that castor oil delivers.

This book explains how to utilize castor oil to promote hair growth and strengthen the roots.
- How to use castor oil to cure dandruff and dry scalp.
- Simple, efficient hair masks that restore luster and vitality to dull, damaged hair.

Castor oil's ability to penetrate deep into the scalp and nourish the hair follicles makes it an indispensable tool for anyone trying to improve their hair's health naturally. We'll go over step-by-step directions for using the oil, how often to use it, and how to construct personalized treatments based on your individual needs.

Castor Oil for Holistic Well-being: Stress Reduction and Sleep Improvement

While castor oil is well-known for its benefits in skincare, hair care, and digestive health, its potential as a holistic stress reliever and sleep enhancer should not be neglected.

Stress and a lack of sleep are two related disorders that can have a negative impact on all aspects of our health. Castor oil's ability to promote relaxation, alleviate tension, and calm the nervous system makes it a natural, gentle solution to these difficulties.

Castor oil can be used in self-care routines such as massage, castor oil packs, and aromatherapy to relax both the body and the mind. Its powerful anti-inflammatory effects aid in the decrease of physical tension, while its deep-penetrating nature promotes relaxation, preparing the body for comfortable sleep. Castor oil, whether taken alone or in combination with relaxing essential oils, is a safe and effective strategy to reduce stress improve sleep quality—two vital aspects of a healthy lifestyle.

Castor Oil for Home Use: A Natural and Eco-Friendly Solution.

Castor oil has practical applications in the home in addition to its health and beauty benefits. As more individuals look for environmentally friendly alternatives to chemical-laden cleaning solutions, castor oil offers a safe, natural answer for home care.

This book explains how castor oil can be used to create non-toxic cleaning agents, reducing exposure to harsh chemicals in your home. It also includes recipes for homemade polishes and furniture care, making it a valuable addition to your household toolkit. Also, it serves as a natural pest deterrent, providing a safe and chemical-free way to manage common household pests.

By incorporating castor oil into your daily routine, you not only improve your health but also contribute to a more sustainable, environmentally friendly lifestyle.

As you read *The Castor Oil Bible*, you will notice an ongoing theme: simplicity. Castor oil is a simple product, and the procedures for using it are easy to understand. This is intentional, as i believe that true wellbeing should be simple to comprehend. It should be easy to include into your daily routine, without the need for a product cabinet or a lengthy ingredient list.

The goal of this guide is to make it simple for you to incorporate natural wellness into your everyday routine with a single, effective product.
Castor oil is adaptable, effective, and proven, and by the end of this book, you will be given the knowledge and confidence to use it to improve your health and beauty from inside.

I hope that this journey will not only introduce you to the insane advantages of castor oil, but also inspire you to take on a more natural, sustainable approach to wellness— one that highlight simplicity, effectiveness, and long-term health.

The History of Castor Oil

Castor oil, obtained from the seeds of the *Ricinus communis* plant, is one of the most traditional natural treatments known to man. Its journey through history reflects not only its effectiveness, but also its broad cultural significance. The oil has been used in traditional medical treatments, religious rites, and even early industrial purposes. To truly understand the historical importance of castor oil today, we must go back in time and trace its origins across civilizations.

The Origins: Ancient Egypt and the earliest uses

The use of castor oil can be traced back as far as ancient Egypt, one of the most advanced and medically knowledgeable civilizations of the ancient world. Castor oil's first documented use dates back to Egypt, where it was valued for its therapeutic benefits. The seeds of the Ricinus communis plant, also known as "kiki" in ancient Egypt, were used as early as 4000 B.C.

Castor oil served many purposes for the Egyptians. It was mostly employed as a laxative, but its applications were far broader. Physicians at the time advised it for skin diseases, and its oil was used as a burn and wound balm. Castor oil was also used in religious and spiritual practices, as it was thought to help treat both bodily and spiritual diseases. Furthermore, it was a beauty regimen mainstay, recognized for promoting healthy, shiny hair. The ancient Egyptians valued their appearance, and castor oil was an important part of their grooming routine, with Cleopatra reportedly using it to improve her physical appearance.

In addition to its therapeutic properties, castor oil has a practical use as a lamp oil, taking advantage of its high burning temperature. Castor oil lamps were common in temples, where the oil's long life as a fuel source made it a valuable resource. This varied application of castor oil in ancient Egypt is one of the first demonstrations of the oil's adaptability and long-lasting appeal.

Furthermore, castor oil was used in the mummification procedure to preserve the corpses. Egyptian embalmers mixed it with oils and resins to seal the bodies of the deceased. This ritual demonstrates the Egyptians' high regard for the oil, both for its worldly advantages and for its function in the afterlife.

India: Ayurveda & Castor Oil's Healing Properties

Around the same time, ancient civilizations in India also started using it. Ayurveda, an Indian traditional system of medicine, used castor oil in a variety of therapies, many of which are still in use today.

In Ayurvedic medicine, castor oil is considered a "cooling" oil, making it suitable for healing imbalances in the body produced by excess heat, or "*pitta*." It was and continues to be used as a strong purgative to cleanse the digestive tract, a procedure that is still used in modern detox regimens. However, Ayurveda recommends castor oil for external usage, notably to relieve joint discomfort and inflammation. The oil is frequently massaged into the skin to relieve arthritis, gout, and muscle stiffness.

Ayurvedic practitioners also used castor oil in cosmetic treatments. It was believed to encourage hair growth, cure dandruff, and improve skin tone. In fact, many traditional Ayurvedic beauty procedures that include castor oil have found their way into modern holistic beauty treatments.

India, like Egypt, recognized castor oil's versatility beyond health and beauty. Its long-lasting properties made it valuable in the production of soaps, ointments, and even as a lubricant for metal tools in early Indian industry. The Indian subcontinent continues to be one of the world's top producers of castor oil, reflecting the region's long history with it.

Greece and Rome: Castor Oil in Classical Medicine

Castor oil spread across Europe mainly through trade and cultural interchange with the Greeks and Romans. The renowned Greek physician Hippocrates, widely considered as the father of modern medicine, recognized the oil's potential and wrote about its purgative characteristics in his medical texts. Hippocrates, who stressed natural remedies and dietary changes in his therapeutic methods, recommended castor oil as a crucial treatment for constipation and other digestive problems.

Pliny the Elder[1], a Roman naturalist, wrote about castor oil in his encyclopedic work Natural History around 77 A.D. He accepted its use as a laxative and a therapy for skin conditions such as warts and cysts. Pliny also described castor oil's early function in women's health, when it was used to induce delivery or manage menstruation. The use of castor oil in this role is one of the first recognized links between the oil and gynecological health, a relationship that is still evident in modern alternative medicine.

Both Greek and Roman civilizations, like those that came before them, valued castor oil's versatile applications. The oil was utilized in early skincare treatments to alleviate rashes and soften the skin. It was also useful in agriculture, where farmers used castor seeds to prevent moles and insects. Castor oil's pest-repelling capabilities were known even then, and the practice is still used in modern organic agricultural systems.

Africa: Castor oil in Traditional African Medicine

In Africa, castor oil has long been used in traditional medicine. Throughout numerous locations and tribes, the oil was utilized for its anti-inflammatory effects and applied to wounds, ulcers, and skin infections. In some African societies, castor oil was thought to have spiritual properties and was used in rituals to purify the body and soul.

---

1 (Pliny the Elder, Plin. Nat. 23.41)

Castor oil was widely used in traditional African medicine, particularly in midwifery. Women would consume castor oil to induce labor, a practice that continues in some communities today. Because of its potential to promote uterine contractions, the oil has become a popular choice among women who want to manage childbirth or post-labor rehabilitation without using modern medications.

Castor oil was also employed in African beauty treatments, as it had been in ancient Egypt and India. Women used it to moisturize their hair and skin, helping to protect them from the harsh, dry weather seen in many parts of Africa. It was also used to make cosmetics and personal care items, a custom that is still practiced by women who want natural beauty treatments.

The Americas: From Native Tradition to Modern Times

When Europeans began exploring the Americas, they took castor oil with them, which quickly incorporated into indigenous medical practices. Native American tribes used castor oil for both medicinal and spiritual purposes, adding it to their extensive list of herbal treatments. It was mostly used to heal skin illnesses, digestive problems, and even as a treatment for snake bites and wounds.

By the 18th and 19th centuries, castor oil had become a colonial American household staple. It was largely used as a laxative, but it was also used to cure a wide range of diseases, including colds and parasite infections. Its importance in households expanded, particularly as people experimented with new uses for the oil. Farmers, for example, utilized castor oil to lubricate machinery, while homeowners discovered it beneficial for preserving leather products and protecting hardwood surfaces.

During the early twentieth century, castor oil was even used in industrial growth. Its application in the manufacture of soaps, varnishes, and even engine lubricants made it a lucrative commodity. It was especially important in aviation during World War I, when castor oil was used to lubricate rotary engines. This signified a transition in castor oil's relevance—it was no longer just a traditional treatment for health and wellness, but it also had a place in industrial and technical progress.

Castor Oil's Decline and Resurgence in Modern Times

By the mid-twentieth century, the advent of synthetic drugs and chemical-based products had led to a decline in the usage of traditional therapies such as castor oil. As pharmaceutical companies created new medications and treatments, many of castor oil's traditional applications were ignored or relegated to the margins.

However, in recent decades, there has been a renewed interest in castor oil, stimulated by a growing demand for natural, organic products. People are rediscovering its benefits, not just in conventional applications, but also in new ones tailored to modern lifestyles. The clean beauty movement, the emergence of holistic health practices, and a desire to return to more sustainable living have all helped to bring castor oil back into the spotlight.

Castor oil is now praised for its wide range of applications and its therapeutic benefits, with fresh studies highlighting the importance of this ancient cure in modern wellness practices.

The Science Behind Castor Oil

This chapter will give you an Overview of Scientific Research and Studies Supporting Castor Oil's Health and Wellness Benefits

For thousands of years, castor oil has been utilized as a natural cure for a number of health problems. Modern science is finally catching up with ancient wisdom, and numerous studies are confirming the traditional uses of castor oil.

While most of the scientific literature is still being developed, existing research provide promising evidence of castor oil's efficacy in skin care, pain reduction, and digestive health.

Ricinoleic Acid: The Secret Behind Castor Oil's Healing Properties

The key component that identifies castor oil from other natural oils is its high concentration of ricinoleic acid, a fatty acid that accounts for approximately 90% of the oil. This unusual molecule is responsible for the majority of the oil's anti-inflammatory, antibacterial, and hydrating qualities. A study [2]published in the *Journal of Pharmacology and Experimental Therapeutics* investigated how ricinoleic acid activates sensory receptors in the body, lowering pain and inflammation.

---

2 (Vieira C. E., *Ricinoleic acid, a specific agonist of capsaicin receptor, induces hyperalgesia in guinea-pigs.*, 2002)

Ricinoleic acid has been found to alleviate pain and inflammation by activating receptors (known as EP3 receptors) in the skin and underlying tissues. This is very useful for treating arthritis, muscle soreness, and joint pain. Ricinoleic acid's anti-inflammatory action is extensively documented in scientific literature, making castor oil an efficient natural pain reliever.

Scientific Evidence for Traditional Use

Castor oil has traditionally been used to moisturize and treat the skin. Its thick nature allows it to establish a barrier on the skin, retaining moisture and soothing inflammation. Modern research backs up these claims, demonstrating that castor oil not only moisturizes but also promotes cellular skin restoration. According to a study published in the *International Journal of Trichology3*, castor oil can increase the production of collagen and elastin, which are essential for maintaining healthy skin.

Additionally, castor oil has antibacterial qualities that aid in the battle against bacteria and fungi, making it a useful therapy for small wounds, burns, and some skin infections. Its ability to reduce inflammation while also protecting the skin from infection makes it ideal for treating acne, eczema, and psoriasis.

The benefits and practical application of castor oil for skin treatment will be covered in the following chapter of this book.

---

3 (Verallo-Rowell, Novel antibacterial and emollient effects of coconut and castor oil on human skin. , 2008)

Digestive Health: Castor Oil as a Natural Laxative

One of the most well-documented applications for castor oil is as a natural laxative. This effect has been used for millennia, but contemporary science has only lately begun to understand how castor oil functions in this capacity.

When ingested, castor oil stimulates the small intestine, causing prostaglandins to be released and intestinal muscles to move more. This helps to ease constipation and encourages bowel movements.

A clinical trial published in *The Journal of Clinical Gastroenterology*4 indicated that castor oil was beneficial in treating chronic constipation, especially as a short-term intervention. The study found that castor oil works swiftly and effectively, providing a natural alternative to over-the-counter laxatives without the associated adverse effects.

When consumed, castor oil interacts with the lining of the small intestine, promoting peristalsis—the rhythmic contraction of intestinal muscles that transport waste through the digestive tract. Ricinoleic acid binds to certain receptors in the intestinal lining, stimulating contractions and causing bowel motions within a few hours of consumption.

Castor oil is normally given orally in tiny doses to treat occasional constipation. The suggested dosage for adults is usually between 1-2 tablespoons.

Castor oil should be used with caution and not as a long-term treatment for digestive disorders, since excessive use can result in consequences such as dehydration.

---

4 (Tournier, 2006)

Promoting Gut Health

Aside from its usage as a laxative, castor oil may benefit overall gut health by improving digestion and lowering inflammation in the digestive tract. Chronic digestive problems, such as irritable bowel syndrome (IBS) or inflammatory bowel disease (IBD), can be caused by gut inflammation, and castor oil's anti-inflammatory qualities can help alleviate the discomfort.

Reducing Inflammation

Ricinoleic acid found in castor oil has been demonstrated[5] to reduce inflammation throughout the body, including the gut. Castor oil may help those with inflammatory digestive disorders by relaxing the intestinal lining and aiding healing.

Digestive Cleansing

Castor oil is occasionally used in detoxification programs to cleanse the digestive tract. Its powerful purgative effects aid in the elimination of waste and pollutants, making it a popular choice for natural cleansing programs.

Soothing digestive discomfort

Castor oil has also been shown to assist relieve occasional digestive pain, such as bloating and cramps. Its ability to accelerate digestion and reduce constipation can lessen the stress and discomfort that are frequently connected with digestive disorders. Applying a warm castor oil compress to the abdomen can provide digestive comfort by increasing circulation and relaxing the intestinal muscles.

---

5 (Swenson P. S., 1990)

Castor Oil Packs for Digestive Health:

Soak a cotton cloth in warm castor oil before placing it over the belly. Cover the cloth with plastic wrap and use a heating pad for 30-60 minutes. This approach reduces stomach cramps and improves digestion by increasing blood flow to the area.

Safety Considerations

While castor oil can be highly effective for relieving constipation, it should be used with caution. It is considered a strong laxative, and overuse can lead to dehydration, cramping, and imbalances in electrolytes. For individuals with chronic digestive issues, it's advisable to consult a healthcare professional before using castor oil as part of a treatment plan.

Anti-inflammatory and pain-relieving properties.

As previously stated, the major component of castor oil, ricinoleic acid, has strong anti-inflammatory properties.
A research published in *Phytotherapy Research*[6] found castor oil can lower inflammation in illnesses like arthritis. The study found that topical use of castor oil helped to relieve pain and increase mobility in patients with joint discomfort, most likely due to its capacity to penetrate deeply into tissues and reduce inflammation at the source.

Castor oil packs, a traditional treatment for joint and muscle discomfort, are also gaining popularity in scientific research. These packs consist of soaking a cloth in warm castor oil and applying it to the affected area.

---

[6] *(Sevastre, The anti-inflammatory and anti-nociceptive effects of castor oil on experimental models. , 2011)*

Castor Oil to Treat Arthritis and Joint Pain

Ricinoleic acid's anti-inflammatory properties, combined with castor oil's ability to permeate deeply into tissues, make it a useful natural therapy for reducing joint stiffness, swelling, and discomfort.

Castor oil can be massaged directly into the afflicted joints to relieve distress. Some people use castor oil packs to provide comfort, which involve soaking a cloth in heated castor oil, laying it over the painful joint, and providing heat for 30-60 minutes. This approach allows the oil to permeate deeper into the tissues, improving circulation and lowering inflammation.

Why it works: The heat from the pack increases circulation, while ricinoleic acid in castor oil relieves inflammation. This combination reduces joint stiffness and improves mobility, making it especially effective for people with rheumatoid arthritis or osteoarthritis.

Muscle soreness and recovery

Castor oil is also commonly used to treat muscle soreness, particularly following physical exertion or injury. Castor oil's anti-inflammatory effects aid to relieve painful muscles, reduce swelling, and speed up healing.

Apply castor oil to painful muscles following exercise or injury. Warm the oil slightly before applying it for optimal absorption and efficiency. Adding a few drops of essential oils, such as peppermint or eucalyptus, can boost the relaxing impact and provide extra pain relief.

Why It Works: Castor oil reduces muscle inflammation while improving blood flow to the affected area, hence promoting muscle repair. Its thick consistency also acts as a lubricant during massage, which helps to relax stiff muscles.

Castor oil for back pain and sciatica.

Lower back pain and sciatica are common problems that can be difficult to treat, resulting in chronic suffering. Castor oil's ability to relieve inflammation and enhance circulation makes it an effective treatment for these conditions.

To relieve back pain or sciatica, apply a castor oil pack to the lower back or affected area. Lie down with the pack in place for 30-60 minutes, letting the warmth and oil to soak into the muscles and tissues.

Why It Works: The combination of warmth and ricinoleic acid relaxes tense muscles, reduces inflammation around the sciatic nerve, and promotes healing. Regular application of castor oil packs can help relieve chronic back pain and improve mobility over time.

Managing Inflammation Following Injury.

Castor oil can also be used to relieve inflammation[7] and swelling following injuries such as sprains, strains, or bruising. Applying castor oil to the wounded region can help to minimize swelling and speed up healing.

To relieve inflammation, gently massage castor oil into the wounded region several times daily. Castor oil packs can help with more serious injuries by boosting circulation and lowering swelling.

Why It Works: Castor oil's anti-inflammatory and analgesic qualities make it useful for treating acute inflammation produced by injury. Castor oil aids in the removal of inflammatory byproducts by boosting blood flow and lymphatic drainage, thereby speeding up healing.

---

7 *(McGarey D. &., 2001)*

Castor Oil's Use in Chronic Inflammatory Conditions

Chronic inflammatory disorders, such as fibromyalgia and inflammatory bowel disease, can result in ongoing pain and discomfort. **While castor oil can not cure these ailments**, its anti-inflammatory properties may help control symptoms and improve quality of life.

How It Helps: Castor oil packs are frequently used as part of comprehensive treatment strategies for chronic inflammation. Castor oil can assist reduce swelling and provide short pain relief.

Why It Works: Castor oil can benefit people with chronic diseases by soothing inflammation and relaxing tense muscles, improving comfort and movement. Its mild, natural approach makes it a popular choice for anyone looking for complementary therapies to treat chronic pain.

The Lymphatic System and Immune Health

The lymphatic system plays a critical role in immune function. It acts as a drainage system for the body, transporting waste products, toxins, and immune cells. The lymph nodes, scattered throughout the body, filter lymphatic fluid, trapping and neutralizing harmful substances like bacteria and viruses.

When the lymphatic system is sluggish or congested, it can compromise the body's ability to eliminate toxins and fight infections.

Castor oil has also been examined for its potential to help the lymphatic system, which is essential for detoxification and immunological function. The lymphatic system transports waste materials, poisons, and immune cells throughout the body. When this system is sluggish or congested, toxins can accumulate and decrease the immune response.

Castor oil packs have been demonstrated to increase lymphatic flow, which improves the body's ability to cleanse and supports immunological health. According to a research published in the *Journal of Naturopathic Medicine8*, using castor oil packs on a regular basis increased lymphatic circulation and reduced swelling in individuals with lymphatic congestion.

Overall, castor oil supports the body's natural defenses in several ways. Whether it's improving lymphatic flow, promoting detoxification, or reducing inflammation, castor oil helps create the conditions necessary for optimal immune function. By incorporating castor oil into your wellness routine, you can give your body the support it needs to stay resilient and healthy.

In addition to using castor oil packs for lymphatic stimulation, castor oil can be massaged onto areas of the body where inflammation or pain is present. Its natural anti-inflammatory properties help to relieve discomfort while supporting the immune system's ability to fight off infections and heal tissues.

Castor oil is also effective against bacteria and fungi. Several studies have shown that castor oil successfully inhibits the growth of bacteria, fungi, and even viruses. *A study published in the Journal of Applied Microbiology9* revealed castor oil to be particularly efficient against Candida albicans, the fungus responsible for yeast infections.

The study found that castor oil could be utilized as a natural alternative to traditional antifungal treatments, especially for people looking for non-toxic, plant-based solutions. Furthermore, the oil's natural capacity to reduce inflammation supports its use in infection treatment and skin healing.

---

8 *(McGarey M. , 1993)*

9 *(Swenson P. S., 1990)*

Supporting Hormonal Balance

Hormonal balance is critical for overall health, influencing everything from energy and mood to metabolism and reproduction. Hormonal imbalances can cause a variety of disorders, including menstruation irregularities, menopause symptoms, thyroid problems, and even emotional disturbances.

Many people turn to natural therapies to maintain hormonal balance, and castor oil has emerged as an effective tool in this regard.

With its effects on the lymphatic system, liver function, and circulation, can help to improve the body's hormonal balance, making it a flexible addition to natural health routines.

The relationship between hormonal health and detoxification

Castor oil helps with the body's natural detoxification processes, which is one of the most important ways it supports hormonal health. Toxin buildup, particularly in the liver, which processes and metabolizes hormones, is a common cause of hormonal abnormalities.

The liver is responsible for breaking down and eliminating excess hormones such as estrogen. When the liver's function is weakened or sluggish, these hormones can build, causing hormonal imbalance symptoms such as weariness, mood swings, and irregular menstruation cycles.

Castor oil, when taken in the form of a castor oil pack, stimulates liver function and aids in the detoxification process. This, in turn, helps to regulate hormone levels by encouraging the efficient breakdown and removal of excess hormones. Castor oil improves lymphatic drainage and circulation, which aids in the clearance of metabolic waste products and promotes overall hormonal health.

Castor Oil and Estrogen Dominance

Estrogen dominance is a frequent hormonal imbalance, particularly in women, in which there is an excess of estrogen relative to other hormones such as progesterone. This disorder can cause a number of symptoms, such as heavy or irregular menstruation cycles, bloating, weight gain, and mood swings. Castor oil can help manage estrogen dominance by improving liver health and increasing the body's ability to handle and eliminate excess estrogen.

How it helps: When administered as a castor oil pack to the liver, it stimulates circulation and lymphatic movement, promoting the cleansing process. This can be especially beneficial for women with estrogen dominance because it helps the body process and remove excess estrogen.

Hormone-related benefits: Regular usage of castor oil packs has been shown to alleviate symptoms of hormonal imbalances such as PMS, irregular periods, and bloating. While additional research is needed to completely understand the link, anecdotal evidence and historic use support the use of castor oil to treat hormone-related illnesses.

Supporting Reproductive Health and Menstrual Relief

Castor oil has traditionally been used to promote female reproductive health. Its anti-inflammatory and purifying characteristics make it an effective natural treatment for menstruation pain, irregular periods, and disorders including ovarian cysts and fibroids. Castor oil can help reduce pain and improve reproductive health by increasing circulation and decreasing inflammation.

Menstrual pain and cramps.

One of the most prominent10 uses of castor oil in hormonal health is to relieve menstruation cramps. The anti-inflammatory qualities of ricinoleic acid, the major fatty acid in castor oil, aid in reducing inflammation and muscular contractions associated with painful periods.

How to use it: Apply a warm castor oil pack on the lower abdomen for 30-60 minutes during menstruation. The warmth of the pack, along with the calming effects of castor oil, can help relax uterine muscles and relieve cramps.

Why it works: Castor oil improves blood flow to the pelvic area, hence reducing congestion and inflammation. This can not only relieve pain, but also improve menstrual flow.

Ovarian cysts and fibroids.

Ovarian cysts and uterine fibroids are hormonal disorders that can cause discomfort, irregular bleeding, and pain. Castor oil packs are commonly used as a natural therapy to treat these disorders because they stimulate detoxification and reduce inflammation in the reproductive organs.

How to Use It: Applying castor oil packs to the belly on a regular basis will improve circulation and lymphatic drainage, reducing cysts and fibroids. Castor oil packs should not be used during menstruation or pregnancy, as they can enhance circulation to the pelvic area.

---

10 *(Kazemzadeh, 2017)*

Hormonal Balance During Menopause.

Menopause is a substantial hormonal change that is frequently accompanied by symptoms such as hot flashes, nocturnal sweats, mood swings, and weariness. Castor oil's capacity to aid in detoxification and reduce inflammation makes it an effective tool for treating menopausal symptoms.

Applying castor oil[11] packs to the belly can balance hormone levels and improve liver detoxification, perhaps reducing hot flashes and mood swings. Castor oil's relaxing qualities may also provide emotional comfort during this transitional period.

Menopause hormone imbalances can affect sleep patterns, resulting in insomnia or restless nights. Castor oil, when combined with relaxing essential oils like lavender or chamomile, can be massaged into the feet or abdomen to encourage relaxation and better sleep quality.

Thyroid Health with Castor Oil

The thyroid gland regulates hormones that influence metabolism, energy levels, and overall well-being. Thyroid disorders, such as hypothyroidism and hyperthyroidism, can disturb hormonal balance, resulting in fatigue, weight gain or loss, and mood fluctuations. Castor oil may improve[12] thyroid health by increasing circulation, decreasing inflammation, and encouraging detoxification.

How It Works: Applying castor oil packs to the thyroid gland in the neck helps improve circulation and lymphatic drainage, thereby improving thyroid function. Some holistic practitioners advocate castor oil for reducing thyroid inflammation and promoting hormonal balance.

11 (Venzke, 2008)
12 (Ghadiri, 2012)

Castor oil improves circulation and lymphatic drainage, allowing the thyroid gland to function more efficiently.

While there is little scientific evidence on castor oil's direct impact on thyroid health, many people have experienced beneficial results after including it into their holistic thyroid care regimens.

Castor Oil as a Holistic Hormone Support

Castor oil's involvement in supporting hormonal balance comes from its ability to induce detoxification, reduce inflammation, and improve circulation. By promoting liver function and lymphatic drainage, can help regulate hormone levels and relieve symptoms of hormonal imbalances such as menstruation pain, thyroid difficulties, and menopausal discomfort.

While castor oil is not a cure-all for hormone issues, its gentle and natural approach makes it an excellent supplement to any holistic health regimen.

Whether you're dealing with menstruation irregularities, thyroid imbalances, or menopausal symptoms, castor oil is a safe, effective, and time-tested way to support overall hormonal health.

Holistic Wellness

In today's world, the problems of managing stress and maintaining quality sleep have become frequent concerns. Stress has an enormous effect on our physical health in alongside our mental and emotional well-being. Similarly, sleep disorders might impair cognitive performance and immunological response. As individuals increasingly seek natural solutions for modern problems, castor oil has emerged as a useful tool for inducing relaxation, stress reduction, and promoting sleep quality.

While castor oil is most known for its use in beauty and as a digestive aid, its ability to promote health in general is less widely recognized. In this chapter, we'll look at castor oil's lesser-known benefits, including its ability to help you manage stress and improve your sleep. Castor oil, when combined with traditional techniques and modern applications, can help people live more balanced and restful lives.

Castor oil can help with stress and sleep.

Before diving into the specific applications of castor oil, it's important to know the science of stress and sleep and how they interact with our bodies. Stress is our bodies' natural response to perceived threats, resulting in the release of cortisol and other stress chemicals.

While short-term stress can be beneficial in emergency situations, persistent stress can cause damage on our neurological system, resulting in anxiety, high blood pressure, digestive problems, and disrupted sleep patterns.

Sleep, on the other hand, is our body's restorative mechanism. During sleep, the body repairs tissues, analyzes information, and regulates hormone levels. Unfortunately, stress is one of the most dangerous disruptive factors of sleep, triggering a vicious cycle in which poor sleep exacerbates stress and vice versa.

Castor oil, with its particular blend of fatty acids, anti-inflammatory effects, and capacity to improve circulation, can aid in regaining a state of equilibrium From topical applications to relaxing rituals, it has the power to help the body relax, recover, and revitalize.

Improve Sleep with Castor Oil: Natural Support for Restful Nights.

Quality sleep is necessary for general health, but it can be difficult to get when we are stressed or anxious. Castor oil, with its relaxing and calming characteristics, can be a useful natural cure for improving sleep habits.

One of the simplest ways to incorporate castor oil into your sleep routine is to apply it to your skin before bedtime. This not only provides a calming routine, but it also allows you to unwind after a hard day.

How to Use: Before going to bed, gently massage a little amount of castor oil into your feet, hands, or scalp. These points are known in reflexology to be connected to the nervous system, and applying castor oil to them can help you relax. For an extra touch, mix castor oil with a few drops of lavender essential oil, which is known for its ability to relax the mind and encourage sleep.

Why it works: Simply massaging castor oil into your skin promotes circulation and relieves tension. This tells your body that it's time to relax. Lavender oil improves this impact by working on the neurological system to generate a sense of calm.

Castor Oil and Stress Relief: Balancing Your Nervous System

One of the most devastating effects of prolonged stress is the toll it takes on the nervous system. When our nervous system is always in "fight or flight" mode, we suffer a number of unpleasant symptoms, including irritation, tension headaches, muscle tightness, and increased heart rate. Holistic stress treatment seek to calm the nervous system, helping the body return to a state of equilibrium.

Castor oil can play an important part in this process. When applied topically, it improves circulation and reduces inflammation.
Massaging castor oil into the body stimulates the lymphatic system, facilitating the release of toxins that may be contributing to stress and tension.

Castor Oil Massage: Relieving Tension and Increasing Relaxation

Massage is an effective way to use castor oil to ease tension. Its thick consistency and rich texture make it suitable for deep tissue massage, which helps to relieve muscle tension and promote relaxation.

How to Use: Place the bottle of castor oil in a basin of boiling water to warm it slightly. Then, using strong but light pressure, massage the oil into the areas of your body that carry the most stress, which are often the neck, shoulders, and back.

You can improve this experience by adding a few drops of essential oils with relaxing effects, such as lavender, chamomile, or sandalwood.

Why It Works: Massage improves blood circulation and relaxes muscles by releasing endorphins, your body's natural stress reliever. Castor oil's nutritious properties also soothe the skin, adding to the overall sense of comfort and well-being.

Regular castor oil massage can help to build a relaxing ritual that promotes both physical and emotional release. Even a quick 10-15 minute massage before bed will help you relax and prepare for a good night's sleep.

Castor oil packs for stress relief: An established tradition.

Castor oil packs are an old therapy that provides a variety of health advantages, including stress reduction. This technique involves soaking a cloth in castor oil and applying it to specific parts of the body to aid in cleansing and relaxation.

How to Make a Castor Oil Pack: Soak a clean, soft towel in warmed castor oil. Apply the cloth to your abdomen or lower back, then wrap it in plastic wrap to prevent stains. Place a heating pad or hot water bottle over the area and rest for 30-60 minutes, allowing the oil to sink deeply into your tissues.

Close your eyes and practice deep breathing or meditation while the pack works to calm even more.

Why It Works: The mild warmth, along with castor oil's anti-inflammatory characteristics, helps to relax the nervous system.

The packs are frequently placed on the liver to aid in detoxifying, which is especially effective when stress has produced digestive problems or gut tension.

Regular usage of castor oil packs can improve your body's stress tolerance by promoting calm from inside.

Castor Oil and Aromatherapy: The Best Combination for Sleep Support

When coupled with essential oils, castor oil becomes a potent aid in the holistic treatment of sleep disorders. Many people find it beneficial to mix castor oil with relaxing essential oils like lavender, chamomile, or cedarwood. These essential oils are proven to produce deep relaxation and improve sleep quality.

How to Use It: To make a soothing sleep balm, combine a teaspoon of castor oil with a few drops of your favorite essential oil. Just before going to bed, massage this blend into your pulse points—your wrists, temples, and behind your ears. Inhaling the peaceful aroma of the essential oil while applying the castor oil will activate your body's relaxation response, preparing you for a good night's sleep.

Why It Works: Essential oils have been shown to interact with the limbic system in the brain, which regulates emotions and stress. When paired with castor oil's capacity to moisturize and soothe the skin, this blend can help you relax both physically and mentally.

Castor Oil Promotes Eye Health and Sleep

Eye strain and discomfort can lead to poor sleep, especially if you spend a lot of time in front of a screen. Castor oil might help relieve tired, strained eyes, allowing you to relax more successfully at night.

How to Use It: Just before bedtime, gently massage it around the eyes to reduce puffiness and stress

Why It Works: Studies13 have shown that castor oil can reduce eye dryness and irritation, which can interfere with sleep. By reducing this discomfort, you can create a more comfortable environment for a good sleep.

Combining Castor Oil with Other Holistic Practices to Maximize Benefits

While castor oil is extremely beneficial on its own, it can be enhanced when mixed with other holistic treatments. For example, including castor oil into a daily self-care practice that includes meditation, yoga, or mindfulness exercises might result in a potent synergy that reduces stress and improves sleep.

Meditation with Castor Oil

Apply castor oil on your temples or pulse points before beginning your meditation session. Massaging the oil into your skin can become part of your mindfulness practice, bringing you back to the present moment and preparing you to relax.

Yoga and Castor Oil

If you practice yoga, try using castor oil for self-massage after your session. Yoga already helps to relieve tension and calm the mind, and using castor oil massage can improve the physical relaxation and mental clarity you feel after practicing.

---

13 (Goto, 2002)

Deep Breathing with Castor Oil

After rubbing castor oil into your skin, take a few moments to concentrate on your breathing. Inhale gently and deeply, holding for a few seconds before exhaling. This simple exercise, along with the relaxing benefits of castor oil, can quickly lower tension and prepare your body for a good night's sleep.

As we have explored, castor oil's benefits extend far beyond its well-known applications in skincare and hair care. By incorporating this oil into your daily self-care routine, you can naturally reduce stress, calm the nervous system, and create the conditions necessary for quality sleep.

In the next chapter you will find a list of recipes you can try, whether through massage, castor oil packs, or aromatherapy blends, castor oil offers a gentle yet powerful way to promote holistic wellness.

Radiant Skin: Skincare Routines and Remedies

Everyone wants glowing, bright skin, but getting healthy skin requires more than just cosmetic treatments. True skin health requires nurturing and preserving the skin's natural equilibrium. Castor oil, with its high fatty acid content and excellent moisturizing characteristics, has been used for generations as a natural cure to promote healthy, youthful skin.

In this chapter, we'll look at the benefits of castor oil for skincare, how it works, and some simple routines and solutions to incorporate castor oil into your daily skincare routine.

Why Castor Oil Is Good for Skin Health

The chemical nature of castor oil is what makes it beneficial as a skincare solution. Ricinoleic acid, the major component of castor oil, is known for its anti-inflammatory and antibacterial characteristics, making it ideal for treating a variety of skin disorders. In addition, castor oil's thick nature allows it to penetrate deep into the skin, providing long-term hydration and stimulating cell regeneration.

Moisturization and Hydration.

Castor oil is most commonly used in skincare as a moisturizer[14]. Its ability to seal in moisture and prevent water loss from the skin's surface makes it great for treating dry, flaky, or irritated skin.

---

14 (Verallo-Rowell, Castor oil as a hydrating agent for sensitive skin types., 2008)

How It Works: Castor oil produces a protective barrier on the skin, reducing moisture loss while pulling in hydration. Its emollient characteristics assist to soften and retain skin suppleness, decreasing the appearance of fine lines and wrinkles.

For dry skin, use a few drops of castor oil directly to the face after cleansing. It can also be used with lighter oils like jojoba or rosehip oil to create a personalized face oil mixture. Apply before bed as an overnight treatment for a deeply nourishing effect.

Promoting Skin Cell Regeneration.

Castor oil not only moisturizes but also promotes the natural renewal of skin cells. It improves skin texture and reduces aging indicators such as wrinkles and fine lines by promoting the production of collagen and elastin.

The ricinoleic acid in castor oil penetrates deeply into the skin and promotes cell turnover. Regular application can gradually enhance the general tone and firmness of the skin, resulting in a smoother, more youthful complexion.

How to Use It: For an anti-aging therapy, gently massage castor oil into wrinkle-prone regions like the eyes, mouth, and forehead. You may also use it on the neck and décolletage to keep the skin elasticity in these delicate areas.

Treating Acne and Breakouts

Castor oil it also contains antibacterial[15], making it useful for treating acne and outbreaks. Its capacity to kill acne-causing bacteria, along with its anti-inflammatory properties, reduces redness and swelling, resulting in cleaner skin.

---

15 (Vieira C. E., 2000; Swenson P. S., 1990)

How It Works: Castor oil includes ricinoleic acid, which kills acne-causing bacteria like *Propionibacterium acnes*. It also calms sensitive skin, lowering the intensity of outbreaks and preventing scarring.

How to Use It: For acne-prone skin, apply castor oil straight to blemishes or combine it with tea tree oil, a natural antibacterial, to boost acne-fighting effectiveness. Use as a spot treatment or as part of an oil cleansing regimen to unclog pores and eliminate excess oil from the skin.

Skincare Routines using Castor Oil

Incorporating castor oil into your regular skincare routine is straightforward and may be adapted to different skin types and concerns. The following skincare procedures use castor oil to promote healthy, glowing skin.

The Oil Cleaning Method

Oil cleaning is a popular way to remove makeup, grime, and excess oil while keeping the skin hydrated. Castor oil, with its thick texture and capacity to dissolve contaminants, is commonly used as the foundation oil in this procedure.

How To Use It: Combine castor oil and a lighter oil, such as olive or sunflower oil, in a 1:2 ratio (adjust to your skin type). Apply the mixture to your face and gently massage in circular motions for around 2-3 minutes.

Soak a washcloth in warm water, wring it out, and apply it on your face to open your pores. After 30 seconds, wipe the oil from your skin, leaving it clean and nourished.

Why It Works: Unlike standard cleansers, which can strip the skin of natural oils, oil cleansing with castor oil balances oil production, making it suited for all skin types, even oily and acne-prone skin.

Overnight Hydration Treatment.

Castor oil can be used as an intensive overnight treatment to replace moisture and enhance skin suppleness in people who have dry or aging skin. Its thick consistency allows it to be used as a nighttime mask, locking in moisture while you sleep.

How to Use: After cleansing your skin in the evening, apply a thin coating of castor oil to your face and neck. For additional advantages, use castor oil with a few drops of a moisturizing essential oil like lavender or chamomile. Leave it on overnight, then wash your face with a light cleanser in the morning.

Why it works: Overnight treatments allow castor oil to permeate deeply into the skin, sealing in moisture and stimulating collagen formation, resulting in firmer, more radiant skin by morning.

Castor oil for dark circles and puffiness.

Castor oil's anti-inflammatory and moisturizing qualities can help to reduce dark circles and puffiness around the eyes.

How to Use It: Before bed, gently massage a drop of castor oil under each eye. The oil's thick texture hydrates the sensitive skin around the eyes, while its anti-inflammatory properties help to minimize puffiness and dark circles.

Why it works: Castor oil's rich fatty acid content nourishes the delicate skin around the eyes, while its relaxing effects minimize puffiness and enhance circulation.

Treatments for Specific Skin Conditions

Aside from its use in daily skincare routines, castor oil is beneficial in treating particular skin disorders[16]. Castor oil's calming, anti-inflammatory characteristics make it an effective treatment for a wide range of skin conditions, including eczema and sunburn.

Eczema & Psoriasis

Eczema and psoriasis both cause itchy, irritated skin. Castor oil's ability to hydrate and relieve inflammation makes it an effective natural treatment for flare-ups.

How to Use It: Apply castor oil directly to the affected regions and massage gently. For severe situations, combine castor oil with a calming oil such as coconut or almond oil to make a more nourishing mixture. Apply the mixture to the skin twice a day.

Why It Works: Castor oil produces a protective barrier over the skin, preventing moisture loss and relaxing inflammation, thereby reducing itching and discomfort caused by eczema and psoriasis.

Sunburn relief

Castor oil, with its anti-inflammatory and moisturizing characteristics, can help burnt skin heal. It reduces pain and redness while facilitating speedier recovery.

How to Use It: Combine castor oil with aloe vera gel, another natural cure for sunburn, and apply to the affected region. Reapply as needed to alleviate discomfort and improve recovery.

---

16 (Sevastre B. N., 2011)

Why It Works: The moisturizing characteristics of castor oil, along with the cooling impact of aloe vera, assist to soothe burnt skin, reduce inflammation, and promote healing.

Anti-Aging Solutions with Castor Oil

As we age, our skin naturally changes—fine lines emerge, wrinkles deepen, and the skin loses flexibility. While aging is a natural process, many people seek to maintain a youthful, healthy appearance by using remedies that are both effective and friendly on their skin. Castor oil, with its nourishing, moisturizing, and regenerating characteristics, is an effective yet natural treatment for many common indications of aging.

In this chapter, we will look at how castor oil can help minimize the appearance of wrinkles, increase skin elasticity, and promote general skin health as part of an anti-aging skincare regimen.

How Castor Oil Promotes Anti-Aging

The particular makeup of castor oil is what makes it beneficial as an anti-aging remedy. Castor oil, which is high in fatty acids, has powerful moisturizing, anti-inflammatory, and regenerative characteristics which are helpful in the treatment of visible signs of aging. Castor oil also increases the development of collagen and elastin, which are vital proteins that keep the skin tight and elastic.

Moisturizing to prevent wrinkles.

Dry, dehydrated skin is one of the leading causes of wrinkles. As we age, our skin's natural capacity to retain moisture diminishes, resulting in the production of fine lines and deep wrinkles. Castor oil is an excellent natural moisturizer that helps to retain moisture and restore skin smoothness, hence reducing the appearance of wrinkles.

How It Works: Castor oil creates a protective barrier on the skin's surface, reducing water loss and encouraging deep hydration. Its high fatty acid content penetrates the skin's outer layer, giving hydration to the deeper layers.

To hydrate, apply a few drops of castor oil to clean, wet skin. Massage it gently into dry, wrinkle-prone areas like the eyes, mouth, and forehead. Use it as part of your nighttime skincare routine to replenish moisture and minimize the appearance of fine wrinkles.

Increasing Collagen and Elastin Production.

As we age, the body's natural production of collagen and elastin—proteins that give the skin structure and elasticity—begins to diminish. The loss of these proteins causes drooping skin and the creation of wrinkles. Castor oil can help counteract this process by boosting[17] collagen and elastin formation, resulting in firmer, more elastic skin.

How It Works: The ricinoleic acid in castor oil stimulates the formation of collagen and elastin, which helps to keep the skin tight and structural. This impact gradually minimizes the appearance of fine lines and wrinkles while enhancing overall skin texture.

---

17 (Verallo-Rowell, Novel emollient and skin-firming effects of castor oil on aging skin., 2008)

How to Use It: Apply castor oil to sagging regions, such as the jawline, neck, and under the eyes. Gently massage the oil into the skin in upward, circular strokes to promote circulation and absorption. For the best benefits, incorporate it into your daily anti-aging routine.

Smoothing out fine lines and wrinkles.

Castor oil's ability to deeply hydrate and encourage cell regeneration makes it an effective natural therapy for reducing fine lines and wrinkles[18]. Regular application can soften existing wrinkles and prevent new ones from forming by regulating the skin's moisture balance and suppleness.

How It Works: Castor oil penetrates the skin's deepest layers, hydrating from within and stimulating the growth of new cells. This results in a smoother, more youthful complexion over time.

Use castor oil as a spot treatment for fine lines and wrinkles. Apply a few drops straight to the crow's feet, smile lines, and forehead wrinkles. Massage lightly to allow the oil to soak completely. For an extra anti-aging boost, mix castor oil with a few drops of a skin-firming essential oil, such as frankincense or rosehip oil.

Restoring skin elasticity

One of the most visible signs of aging is a loss of skin elasticity, especially around the neck, jawline, and eyes. As the skin loses its capacity to "bounce back," it begins to droop. Castor oil helps to restore suppleness by stimulating collagen formation and moisturizing the skin from within.

---

18 (wenson, 1990)

How It Works: Castor oil's deep penetration and ability to stimulate collagen and elastin formation aid in the restoration of the skin's natural structure and firmness. This can help to reduce the appearance of sagging skin and provide a more youthful, toned look.

How to Use It: Apply castor oil twice a day to regions prone to sagging, such as the neck and under the chin. Massage it in with vigorous upward strokes to lift and tone the skin.

Reducing age spots and hyperpigmentation.

As the skin ages, age spots and hyperpigmentation become more common, which is frequently caused by UV exposure or hormonal changes. Castor oil, with its regenerative characteristics[19], can aid to lighten dark spots and even out skin tone.

How It Works: Castor oil's fatty acids aid to break down excess melanin in the skin, which is responsible for dark spots. Castor oil applied on a regular basis encourages skin rejuvenation, which aids in the fading of age spots and the restoration of an even complexion.

How to Use It: Apply castor oil directly on age spots or hyperpigmented areas once or twice a day. You can also combine castor oil with lemon essential oil, which has brightening effects, to create a more effective treatment. Over time, this approach can help decrease the appearance of age spots and restore the shine of your skin.

---

19 (Sevastre B. N., *Castor oil's effects on sun-damaged skin and its potential for reducing hyperpigmentation.*, 2011)

Healing Sun Damage

Sun exposure contributes significantly to premature aging, resulting in wrinkles, fine lines, and sunspots. Castor oil's high antioxidant content helps to repair and protect the skin from additional sun damage.

How It Works: Castor oil's antioxidants neutralize free radicals, which cause oxidative stress and contribute to skin aging. Castor oil helps protect the skin from potential damage by lowering the influence of free radicals. It also aids in the healing of current sun damage.

How to Use It: In the evening, apply castor oil to sun-damaged areas and leave it on overnight to restore and nourish the skin. Regular use can enhance skin texture and lessen the appearance of sunspots and wrinkles caused by UV radiation.

Adding Castor Oil to Your Anti-Aging Skincare Routine

To maximize castor oil's anti-aging properties, add it into your daily skincare routine. Here are a few important measures for utilizing castor oil properly as part of an anti-aging regimen.

Daily Hydration with Anti-Wrinkle Treatment

Using castor oil as a daily moisturizer keeps skin moisturized and reduces the look of wrinkles. Use it in your morning and evening rituals.

How to Use It: After cleansing your face in the morning, massage a tiny amount of castor oil into your skin, focusing on areas prone to dryness and fine wrinkles. Allow the oil to penetrate before using makeup or sunscreen. Repeat the method in the evening, after cleaning and toning your skin.

Overnight Anti-Ageing Mask

Castor oil can be used as an overnight treatment to provide deep hydration and promote skin regeneration while you sleep, for even greater anti-aging benefits.

How to Use It: Apply a thick layer of castor oil to your face and neck before bedtime. For even more relaxation, add a drop of lavender essential oil. Leave the oil on overnight, then rinse your face in the morning to reveal softer, smoother skin.

Weekly Castor Oil Massage.

Regularly massaging castor oil into your skin helps boost circulation and increase its anti-aging properties.

How to Use It: Apply castor oil on your face, neck, and décolletage in circular motions once or twice a week. This helps to stimulate collagen formation, resulting in firmer, more younger skin.

Sensitive Skin

Individuals with sensitive skin might find it difficult to find skincare solutions that are both effective and gentle. Many commercial products include harsh chemicals that can cause irritation, redness, and breakouts. Castor oil, with its natural moisturizing and anti-inflammatory characteristics, is widely regarded as a safe alternative for sensitive skin when used properly. However, even with a natural product like castor oil, it is important to understand how to use it correctly to minimize undesirable side effects.

In this chapter, we will look at how castor oil can be used to soothe sensitive skin, how to use it safely, and how to avoid irritation while benefiting from the oil's delicate yet powerful characteristics.

Why Castor Oil is Great for Sensitive Skin?

Castor oil contains ricinoleic acid, a fatty acid with anti-inflammatory and antibacterial characteristics, making it suitable for calming sensitive skin without creating discomfort. Castor oil, unlike many synthetic skincare products, interacts with the skin's natural processes to restore balance and protect the barrier. It is also non-comedogenic, which means it will not clog pores, which is extremely helpful for sensitive, acne-prone skin.

Moisturizing without irritation.

Sensitive skin is prone to dryness, and finding a moisturizing lotion that does not cause redness or irritation can be tricky.
Castor oil is exceptionally hydrating, but its thick, viscous consistency can be overwhelming for sensitive skin. The solution is to dilute it with lighter, non-irritant oils or ingredients.

How It Works: Castor oil produces a protective barrier on the skin's surface, limiting moisture loss and nourishing deeper layers. It relieves dryness, flakiness, and irritation, which are common symptoms of sensitive skin.

How to Use It: Combine a few drops of castor oil with a lighter oil, such as jojoba or almond oil, to make a more balanced and easily absorbed blend. Apply this combination to sensitive regions of the face or body, preferably after cleansing, when the skin is most responsive to moisture.

Reducing inflammation and irritation.

Sensitive skin commonly reacts to external stimuli, causing redness, itching, or irritation. Castor oil's anti-inflammatory qualities make it an effective therapy for relieving these flare-ups.

How It Works: Ricinoleic acid, is proven to alleviate inflammation. When applied topically, castor oil soothes inflamed skin, making it ideal for those with eczema or dermatitis.

How to Use It: Apply a tiny amount of diluted castor oil to sensitive skin regions to relieve redness and irritation. Use it as a spot treatment for sensitive skin patches or to massage a little layer into bigger areas of inflammation.

Healing Without Harmfulness

Sensitive skin might take longer to heal from irritations or small injuries, and cosmetics containing harsh chemicals can exacerbate the problem. Castor oil aids speedier healing without adding new irritants.

How It Works: Castor oil promotes wound healing by encouraging the creation of new skin cells and boosting collagen formation. Its antibacterial capabilities assist to keep sensitive skin infection-free while it heals.

How to Use It: Gently apply a tiny amount of castor oil to any small cuts, scratches, or areas of irritation. Ensure that the skin is clean prior to application, and avoid using too much oil, since a thick coating may prevent the skin from breathing.

Tips for Safely Using Castor Oil on Sensitive Skin

While castor oil is generally safe for most skin types, people with sensitive skin should use it with caution. Here are some recommendations for applying castor oil in a way that reduces irritation while optimizing its advantages.

Patch Test Before Full Application

Sensitive skin is more likely to react to new products than other skin types. To avoid bad reactions, always do a patch test before applying castor oil to your face or body.

Patch testing involves applying a small amount of diluted castor oil to a discrete area of the skin, such as behind the ear or on the inner arm. Leave it on for 24 hours and look for signs of redness, itching, and irritation. If no reaction develops, the oil can be safely used in more sensitive regions.

Dilute castor oil with lighter oils.

Castor oil, with its thick and heavy nature, can sometimes seem too rich for delicate skin. Diluting castor oil with lighter, non-comedogenic oils makes it easier for the skin to absorb while lowering the danger of blocking pores or causing irritation.

Recommended Oils for Dilution: Jojoba oil, sweet almond oil, and grapeseed oil are all excellent options for diluting castor oil. These oils are soft, non-irritating, and readily absorbed, making them great for sensitive skin.

Begin by diluting castor oil in a 1:3 ratio with lighter oil. You can alter the ratio to suit your skin's tolerance and unique needs.

Use sparingly.

Castor oil should be used sparingly on sensitive skin. Applying too much castor oil at once might overwhelm delicate skin, resulting in closed pores and discomfort. If your skin tolerates castor oil well, start with a small amount and gradually increase your use.

How to Use: Apply a few drops of diluted castor oil to the skin in gentle, circular strokes. Avoid applying copious coats of oil, particularly to the face. It's finest applied as a little layer before bedtime or as a protective balm for dry, irritated skin.

Avoid daily use at first.

If you're new to castor oil or have really sensitive skin, don't use it every day until you know how your skin reacts. Begin with two or three applications per week, then progressively increase if your skin responds positively.

Why It Matters: Sensitive skin may require time to adjust to new products. By incorporating castor oil gradually into your routine, you allow your skin to develop tolerance without overwhelming it.

Remedies for Common Sensitive Skin Conditions

Castor oil is a natural medicine that can effectively treat common sensitive skin problems like eczema, dermatitis, and rosacea.

Eczema & Dermatitis

Castor oil has anti-inflammatory and hydrating characteristics, making it a gentle yet effective treatment for eczema and dermatitis flare-ups.

How to Use: Apply a diluted mixture of castor and jojoba oil to the afflicted areas twice a day. This reduces redness, itching, and irritation while delivering long-term hydration.

Rosacea

For individuals with rosacea, castor oil can help calm inflammation and redness without causing irritation.

How to Use: Combine castor oil with grapeseed oil and apply a tiny amount to areas of redness and inflammation. Use this therapy at night to relieve flare-ups.

Hair Health: How to improve Hair Health with Castor Oil

Many people want to have strong, healthy hair, but environmental damage, aging, stress, and improper hair care habits can weaken hair strands and cause delayed growth. Castor oil, with its thick consistency and high nutrient content, has long been considered to be an effective natural cure for improving hair health, encouraging growth, and strengthening each hair strand.

In this chapter, we'll look at how to use castor oil to feed your hair, stimulate hair growth, and protect it from harm while staying consistent with your natural wellness routine.

Why is Castor Oil Effective for Hair Health?

The benefits of castor oil for hair health are mostly due to its high concentration of ricinoleic acid, an omega-9 fatty acid with anti-inflammatory, antibacterial[20], and highly moisturizing characteristics. Castor oil also includes key elements such as vitamin E, proteins, and minerals, all of which are necessary for feeding the scalp, promoting hair growth, and improving hair strength and thickness.

Moisturizing: Due to its thick consistency, castor oil may deeply hydrate[21] the scalp and hair, which is especially good for people who have dry, frizzy, or brittle hair. The oil locks in moisture, making strands stronger and less likely to break.
Castor oil contains ricinoleic acid, which promotes blood circulation to the scalp, supporting healthier hair follicles and hair development[22].

---

20 (Swenson P. S., Antimicrobial effects of ricinoleic acid in the treatment of dandruff, 1990)
21 (Sevastre B. N., 2011)
22 (Verallo-Rowell, The role of castor oil in stimulating hair growth and improving scalp health., 2008)

Strengthening Strands: Castor oil protects the hair shaft from environmental damage and reduces split ends, resulting in longer, healthier hair over time.

Castor oil promotes hair growth.

One of the most common use of castor oil is to promote hair growth. Many people who suffer from thinning hair, hair loss, or delayed hair growth turn to castor oil as a natural cure because of its high vitamin content and stimulating properties.

Scalp Massage for Hair Growth

The most effective technique to boost hair development with castor oil is to incorporate it into your daily scalp care routine. Regular scalp massages with castor oil stimulate blood flow to the hair follicles, supplying oxygen and nutrients needed for hair development.

How It Works: Castor oil's ricinoleic acid content improves circulation while its nourishing characteristics provide necessary fatty acids and vitamin E for the scalp. This offers the ideal conditions for hair follicles to develop new, healthy hair.

How To Use It: Warm a tiny amount of castor oil and apply it to the scalp in circular motions for 5-10 minutes. Concentrate on regions where the hair is thinning or where you wish to promote growth. Leave the oil on for at least 30 minutes, or overnight for deeper penetration, before rinsing thoroughly with a gentle shampoo. For optimal results, do this treatment twice to three times each week.

Castor Oil Hair Growth Mask.

Castor oil can be used as the basis for a nourishing hair mask that offers a more intensive hair growth therapy. When paired with other growth-stimulating substances, this mask rejuvenates the scalp and promotes stronger, thicker hair growth.

How It Works: The thick, nutrient-rich consistency of castor oil aids in damage repair and development, while other ingredients such as coconut oil or aloe vera offer moisture and nutrients to support healthy hair growth.

How To Use It: Combine 2 tablespoons castor oil, 1 tablespoon coconut oil (for extra hydration), and 1 tablespoon aloe vera gel (to soothe the scalp). Apply the mixture to your scalp and hair, concentrating on the roots. Cover your hair with a shower cover and let the mask sit for 1-2 hours before rinsing with a light wash. Use this treatment once a week to promote hair growth.

Strengthening Hair with Castor Oil

Castor oil not only promotes growth, but also strengthens individual hair strands, minimizing breakage and broken ends. Castor oil protects the hair shaft from environmental damage, styling tools, and natural wear and tear, which can result in brittle, thin hair.

Deep Conditioning Treatment.

Castor oil is a good choice for a deep conditioning treatment because its thick consistency helps it to penetrate deeply into the hair shaft, trapping in moisture and strengthening the strands from the inside.

How It Works: Castor oil includes vitamin E, which is crucial for repairing and protecting damaged hair. Its fatty acids also aid to seal the hair cuticle, which makes it more resistant to breakage and split ends.

How to Use It: Warm 1-2 tablespoons of castor oil and apply it to the length of your hair, concentrating on the ends where damage is most likely to develop. Comb the oil through your hair to ensure it's evenly distributed. Cover your hair with a shower cap or a warm towel and let the oil sit for 1-2 hours. Rinse well with shampoo. Repeat this deep conditioning treatment once a week to keep your hair strong and healthy.

Repairing split ends

Split ends can be one of the most annoying aspects of hair care since they make hair seem unhealthy and block growth. Castor oil's ability to smooth and seal the hair shaft makes it a natural way to prevent and restore split ends.

How It Works: Castor oil coats the hair's ends to prevent additional splitting and damage. Its moisturizing characteristics also help to maintain the ends of the hair soft and supple, lowering the risk of breaking.

How to Use It: After shampooing and conditioning your hair, add a small amount of castor oil to the ends while still damp. Concentrate on places that are likely to separate. Castor oil can also be used as a leave-in treatment to keep your hair's ends protected all day.

Treating Scalp Health with Castor Oil

Healthy hair development begins with a healthy scalp, and castor oil is an excellent way to keep your scalp healthy. It can help address conditions including dandruff, dryness, and inflammation, all of which can inhibit healthy hair development.

Treatment for Dry Scalp and Dandruff

Dry, flaky scalps can lead to hair thinning and loss. Castor oil's hydrating and antifungal characteristics make it an effective treatment for dandruff and dry scalp.

How It Works: Ricinoleic acid's antifungal characteristics attack yeast and fungi that cause dandruff, while castor oil's deep moisturizing impact relieves dryness and itching.

How to Use It: Massage castor and coconut oil into your scalp and keep it on for at least 30 minutes before shampooing. Regular application of this therapy reduces dandruff and calms scalp irritation.

Soothing an irritated scalp

Scalp irritation from styling products, harsh shampoos, or environmental conditions can weaken hair follicles and prevent development. Castor oil helps relieve itchy scalps, reduce inflammation, and promote a healthier scalp environment.

How It Works: Castor oil's anti-inflammatory effects relieve inflammation and redness, while its antibacterial capabilities keep the scalp clean and infection-free.

How to Use It: Gently massage castor oil into sore regions of the scalp. Leave it on for 30 to 60 minutes before rinsing with a gentle shampoo. For chronic scalp irritation, apply this therapy twice a week.

Protecting the Hair from Damage

Castor oil not only nourishes and moisturizes the hair, but also protects it from environmental and heat damage. The oil creates a protective layer around the hair shaft, mitigating the effects of heat styling equipment, UV exposure, and pollution.

How to Use It: Before using heat styling products, add a tiny amount of castor oil to the length of your hair to prevent it from heat damage. You can also use castor oil to your hair before swimming to protect it from chlorine and seawater.

Safety and Side Effects.

Castor oil has been used for ages as a natural treatment for a variety of health and beauty issues. Its high nutrient content, strong anti-inflammatory qualities, and adaptability have made it a popular choice for skin care, hair health, digestion, and overall wellness. However, like with any natural therapy, it is important to understand its safety profile, potential side effects, and proper application to avoid any negative reactions.

In this chapter, we will look at the safety of castor oil, its potential side effects, and the precautions you should take when using it in your health and beauty routine. While castor oil is typically safe for most people, certain measures must be taken to ensure that it is used properly.

The Overall Safety of Castor Oil

Castor oil is widely recognized as a safe and effective treatment when used correctly. The United States Food and Drug Administration (FDA)[23] has approved it as safe for both topical and oral use, while its oral use is normally reserved for short-term constipation relief due to its severe laxative impact.

---

23 https://www.fda.gov/

Castor oil's natural makeup, which is high in ricinoleic acid, provides significant benefits without the harsh additives present in many commercial formulations.

However, as with any natural oil, people's reactions vary based on their skin type, sensitivities, and pre-existing health concerns. It is important to use caution, particularly when using castor oil for the first time or in big quantities.

Possible Side Effects of Castor Oil

Although castor oil is generally considered safe, some people may experience negative effects, particularly when used incorrectly or in large quantities. Here are some of the most common negative effects related to the usage of castor oil:

Skin reactions.

Castor oil is generally safe to use topically, but in rare circumstances, it might cause allergic reactions or skin irritation, especially in people with sensitive or reactive skin. A skin response can cause redness, itching, and rash.

How to Avoid It: Always conduct a patch test before applying castor oil to wider portions of the skin, especially if you have sensitive skin. To conduct a patch test, apply a little amount of castor oil to an inconspicuous region, such as behind the ear or on the inner arm, and wait 24 hours. If no irritation occurs, it is likely safe for wider use. To lessen the risk of irritation, consider diluting castor oil with lighter oils such as jojoba or almond oil.

Allergic reactions.

While allergic responses to castor oil are infrequent, they do occur. An allergic response may cause swelling, hives, or trouble breathing, especially when castor oil is applied to sensitive areas or used in high doses.

How to Avoid It: If you have a history of adverse reactions to oils or skincare products, get medical advice before using castor oil. If you see any symptoms of an allergic reaction, stop taking the oil right away and seek medical treatment if they are severe.

Clogged Pores

For some sensitive skin types, especially those prone to breakouts, castor oil's thick consistency may lead to clogged pores if used in excess.

How to Avoid: Always dilute castor oil with lighter oils and apply it sparingly. Use it as part of an oil-cleansing routine or overnight treatment, rather than leaving it on the skin throughout the day.

Dryness from Overuse

Interestingly, while castor oil is highly moisturizing, using too much of it, especially without dilution, can sometimes cause the skin to feel dry or tight. This occurs when the oil forms a barrier that prevents moisture from penetrating the skin.

How to Avoid: To prevent dryness, always dilute castor oil with a lighter oil and avoid over-application. If you notice that your skin feels dry after using castor oil, reduce the frequency of use or mix it with a more hydrating oil like almond or argan oil.

Gastrointestinal side effects

Castor oil is an effective laxative when taken orally, activating gut muscle contractions and encouraging bowel motions. While castor oil might help with constipation, ingesting too much can cause unpleasant side effects such as diarrhea, cramps, nausea, and dehydration.

How to Avoid It: When using castor oil as a laxative, strictly follow the dosage directions. The suggested dose for adults is usually between 1 and 2 tablespoons, but this can vary depending on individual needs and tolerance. Never exceed the suggested amount, and do not take castor oil as a laxative for an extended period of time, as it might cause dependency or electrolyte imbalance. If you have severe stomach distress, stop using it right once and see a doctor.

Precautions when using castor oil

In addition to being aware of potential adverse effects, it is important to take specific measures when using castor oil. Proper application can help you avoid unwanted responses while maximizing the oil's advantages.

Pregnancy and breastfeeding.

Pregnant women should be cautious when taking castor oil, especially when eaten. Castor oil has long been used to induce labour due to its ability to trigger uterine contractions. While this effect can be advantageous in certain cases, it can potentially cause issues if taken too early during pregnancy.

Recommendation: Pregnant women should not use castor oil except under the guidance of a healthcare provider. Before using castor oil in any form during pregnancy, check your doctor or gynecologist. While topical treatment is generally regarded safe, it is still best to consult with a healthcare expert.

Internal Use and Dosage.

As previously stated, castor oil is a strong laxative that should be used internally with caution. Long-term usage of castor oil for constipation alleviation can lead to dependence, in which the bowels grow reliant on the oil for proper operation. When taken excessively, it can lead to dehydration and electrolyte abnormalities.

Recommendation: Use castor oil internally only as a short-term constipation treatment. Always follow the suggested dosage and don't use it more than once or twice a week. If constipation persists, ask a doctor about change therapies.

Eye Sensitivity.

While castor oil can help to moisturize and preserve the skin surrounding the eyes, it is important to avoid putting the oil straight into the eyes. Castor oil in the eyes can cause irritation, redness, and blurred vision.

Recommendation: Use a tiny amount of castor oil near the eyes (for example, to diminish dark circles or wrinkles) and gently massage it in with clean hands. If the oil accidently gets into your eyes, rinse gently with water and avoid rubbing the area.

Interactions with medications and essential oils

Castor oil, particularly when used internally, might have an impact on the digestive system, potentially affecting medicine absorption. Its laxative impact might shorten the time drugs spend in the digestive tract, thereby lowering their effectiveness. Furthermore, castor oil's capacity to affect fluid balance and detoxifying processes may complicate interactions with some drugs.

Interaction With Digestive Medications

Castor oil, a potent stimulant laxative, may interact with medicines24 used to regulate bowel movements, such as laxatives or antidiarrheal treatments.

Why It Matters: Combining castor oil with other laxatives raises the risk of dehydration and electrolyte imbalance. Castor oil may interfere with the action of antidiarrheal drugs, causing additional stomach problems.

Precaution: If you are currently using digestive drugs, especially prescription laxatives or antidiarrheals, check your doctor before using castor oil internally. Overuse of laxatives might lead to dependency or other gastrointestinal issues.

Interaction with diuretics

Diuretics, sometimes known as water pills, are used to eliminate excess fluid from the body. Castor oil's laxative effect can cause fluid loss25, therefore combining it with diuretics raises the risk of severe dehydration and electrolyte abnormalities.

Why This Matters: Electrolyte imbalances can cause issues like muscle cramps, tiredness, and abnormal heart rhythms. This is especially dangerous for people who have kidney or cardiac issues.

Precaution: If you are using diuretics, do not use castor oil as a laxative unless authorized by your healthcare provider. To reduce potential fluid loss, limit your use of castor oil to topical skincare and haircare.

---

24 (Muller-Lissner, 2010)

25 (Palmer, 2014)

Interaction with blood pressure medications.

Castor oil's ability to promote dehydration may interfere with blood pressure-lowering medicines. Dehydration can cause a sudden drop in blood pressure, resulting in dizziness or fainting.

Why It Matters: When paired with hypertension drugs, castor oil's laxative impact may exacerbate blood pressure regulation by lowering fluid levels in the body.

Precaution: If you are using high blood pressure medication, do not take castor oil internally unless your healthcare physician has allowed it. If you decide to use castor oil topically, make sure to stay hydrated.

Interaction with Hormonal Medications

Castor oil's laxative properties might also influence hormonal drugs including birth control pills and thyroid treatments. Diarrhea or fast bowel movements might impair the absorption of certain drugs, lowering their effectiveness.

Why It Matters: In the case of oral contraception, inadequate absorption can increase the chance of unwanted pregnancy. Inadequate absorption of thyroid medicines might cause fluctuating hormone levels.

Individuals taking oral contraceptives or thyroid medicines should avoid consuming castor oil internally. If you experience digestive problems, talk to your doctor about possible solutions.

Interaction with blood thinners.

While there is limited evidence of a direct interaction between castor oil and blood thinners, any product that affects digestion or nutrient absorption should be used with caution in people taking anticoagulants.

Why It Matters: Blood thinners like warfarin necessitate close monitoring of nutrient intake, especially vitamin K, which aids in blood clotting. Castor oil-induced digestive problems may impair nutrition absorption26 and compromise clotting factor balance.

Individuals on blood thinners should avoid using castor oil internally unless authorized by a healthcare expert. Regular usage on the skin or hair should not cause problems, but any new supplement should be reviewed with a healthcare expert.

Interactions with Essential Oils

Castor oil is frequently mixed with essential oils to increase therapeutic properties. While these mixtures are generally harmless, certain essential oils may interact with castor oil, enhancing or altering its effects, particularly when taken internally or in high concentration.

Improving Absorption of Essential Oils

Castor oil is a good carrier oil, allowing essential oils to penetrate deeper into the skin. However, its thick nature can inhibit the absorption of some essential oils, resulting in a more gradual effect. This delayed absorption can be useful since it minimizes the possibility of discomfort from strong essential oils such as peppermint or oregano.

---

26 (Suttie, 2009)

How It Works: Castor oil's thick, viscous consistency forms a barrier on the skin, allowing essential oils to be absorbed gradually and lowering the chance of irritation or allergic responses.

 Precaution: Always dilute essential oils with castor oil before application to the skin. To avoid over-concentration, use 1-2 drops of essential oil to each teaspoon of castor oil. Before experimenting with a new combination, do a patch test.

Interaction with photosensitive oils.

Some essential oils, especially citrus oils like lemon or bergamot, are photosensitive, which means they make the skin more sensitive to sunlight. Castor oil combined with photosensitive oils might increase[27] the risk of sunburn or irritation when applied to exposed skin.

How It Works: When castor oil is coupled with photosensitive oils, the essential oil remains on the skin's surface for a longer period of time, increasing the risk of ultraviolet exposure.

Precaution: Do not apply castor oil mixed with photosensitive essential oils before sun exposure. If using citrus-based oils, apply the mixture in the evening and stay out of direct sunshine for at least 12 hours.

Interaction with Strong Antimicrobial Oils.

---

27 (Petersen, 2014)

Certain essential oils, such as tea tree, oregano, and thyme oil, are highly antibacterial. While these oils are frequently used with castor oil for acne treatment or wound care, their potency can occasionally cause skin irritation or dryness, particularly in people with sensitive skin.

How It Works: Castor oil helps to dilute strong essential oils, but some people with sensitive skin may still feel irritation if these oils are applied in large amounts. Always dilute strong essential oils before combining them with castor oil. For sensitive skin, use a 1:5 ratio (one drop of essential oil to five tablespoons of castor oil) and test on a tiny patch of skin before applying the entire amount.

Who should avoid using castor oil?

While castor oil is safe for most people, there are few conditions when its use may not be recommended:

People with Intestinal Blockages or Digestive Disorders: Those who have pre-existing gastrointestinal problems, such as Crohn's disease, ulcers, or intestinal blockages, should avoid using castor oil as a laxative because it may aggravate them.

People with Severe Skin Sensitivity or Allergies: People who are allergic to castor oil or other comparable components should avoid topical usage to avoid allergic reactions.

Safe and Effective Use of Castor Oil.

Castor oil is a highly effective and flexible natural treatment with multiple health and beauty benefits.

However, like any product, it must be used properly to ensure safety and avoid negative consequences. You can enjoy the many benefits of castor oil without having negative side effects if you follow the dosage guidelines, perform patch tests, and take the proper precautions.

As with any new addition to your wellness routine, you should always contact with a healthcare practitioner first, especially if you have any underlying health concerns or allergies. With correct application, castor oil can be a safe, effective, and necessary component of your natural wellness path

Castor Oil Recipes with Essential Oils

Throughout this book, we have explored castor oil's amazing versatility in terms of health, beauty, and overall wellness. Castor oil is a strong natural medicine that has been shown to promote glowing skin and better hair, as well as manage inflammation, pain, and hormonal imbalances. However, when blended with other essential oils, its full potential is amplified. The combination of castor oil and correctly selected essential oils can increase the benefits already mentioned, providing a comprehensive, holistic approach to wellness.

This chapter contains a range of recipes that use castor oil and essential oils to provide powerful, natural treatments for certain health and cosmetic needs. These recipes supplement the remedies you've already heard about, such as increasing skin elasticity, stimulating hair growth, alleviating pain, and encouraging hormonal balance. By incorporating essential oils—each with their own unique properties—into these formulations, we achieve further therapeutic potential, allowing you to customize your approach to your specific needs.

Why Combine Castor Oil and Essential Oils?

Castor oil on its own provides numerous benefits, but essential oils add therapeutic characteristics that might address particular health conditions. Essential oils add an extra layer of healing, whether it's the soothing impact of lavender to relax the skin and mind, the antibacterial activity of tea tree oil to treat blemishes, or the thrilling aroma of peppermint to stimulate hair growth.

Enhanced Absorption: Castor oil's thick, viscous texture functions as a superb carrier oil, allowing essential oils to permeate deeper into the skin and scalp, enhancing their potency.

Targeted Benefits: Essential oils allow you to focus on specific goals, whereas castor oil provides a solid foundation with its hydrating, anti-inflammatory, and healing capabilities. For example, adding rosemary oil to a hair growth treatment boosts circulation, while including frankincense oil into an anti-aging routine stimulates skin regeneration.

Customizable Formulas: The benefit of combining essential oils with castor oil is the opportunity to tailor formulations to your specific preferences and needs. Whether you're looking for an overnight anti-wrinkle serum, a soothing muscle massage, or a scalp treatment to promote hair development, these recipes are versatile.

A holistic approach to wellness

The recipes in this chapter rely on the main knowledge you've received throughout the book, emphasizing a holistic approach to wellbeing. Rather than providing one-size-fits-all answers, these recipes inspire you to customize your self-care regimen by addressing your specific needs with nature's finest ingredients.

Just as castor oil benefits your skin, hair, and overall health, essential oils add a more refined and targeted approach, boosting the healing power of your daily wellness routines. Each recipe is intended to be simple to prepare at home, using simple, natural components that complement the solutions already discussed.

Whether you're new to essential oils or are already familiar with their advantages, this chapter will show you how to make effective, luxurious treatments that not only improve your skin and hair but also boost your mood, quiet your mind, and contribute to a balanced, healthy lifestyle.

General Directions for All Recipes:

1. Measure Ingredients: Start by gathering and measuring the ingredients according to the dosage in each recipe.

2. Mixing: In a small bowl, mix all the ingredients together until they are well combined. You can use a spoon or a small whisk for this.

3. Storage: For recipes that you plan to store, transfer the mixture into an airtight glass jar or container. Store in a cool, dry place or in the refrigerator (depending on the recipe).

4. Application: Apply the mixture to the targeted area as directed (e.g., massage into joints, apply to scalp, or rub on chest). For facial recipes, use clean fingers or a cotton pad for application.

Specific Directions for Recipe Types:

Unless specified otherwise

Anti-Inflammatory and Pain Relief Recipes:

1. Preparation:

   o Warm the castor oil slightly by placing the bottle in a bowl of warm water for a few minutes.

   o Mix in the other oils and essential oils.

2. Application:

   o Gently massage the mixture into the painful or inflamed area.

   o For deeper relief, cover the area with a warm towel or wrap for 15-30 minutes.

   o Use 2-3 times a day, as needed, unless specified otherwise.

3. Storage: Store in a small jar or container and use within 2-3 weeks.

Respiratory Health Recipes:

- o Preparation: Warm the castor oil and mix it with the essential oils.

- o Stir the mixture thoroughly.

2. Application:

- o For chest rubs, massage a generous amount onto the chest, throat, and back before bedtime.

- o You can also inhale the vapors by placing a small amount of the mixture under your nose or by adding a few drops to hot water for steam inhalation.

3. Storage: Store in a dark, airtight container and use within 1-2 months.

Oral and Dental Health Recipes:

1. Preparation:

- o Mix the castor oil with other oils or ingredients like clove oil, tea tree oil, or aloe vera gel.

- o Stir well to ensure all components are blended evenly.

2. Application:

- o For toothache or gum treatments, apply the mixture to a cotton swab or clean finger and gently massage it into the affected area.

- o For mouth rinses, swish the mixture around in your mouth for a minute or two before spitting it out.

- o For canker sores, apply directly to the sore using a cotton swab.

3. Storage: Store the mixture in a cool, dark place and use within 1 month.

Skin and Hair Health Recipes:

1. Preparation:

- o Warm the castor oil slightly before mixing it with other oils like jojoba, argan, or essential oils.

- o Stir or shake well to combine all ingredients.

2. Application:

- o For hair treatments, apply the mixture to your scalp or hair ends and leave it on for 20-30 minutes before washing out.

- o For skin treatments, massage into the skin in a circular motion and leave on for at least 15 minutes before rinsing.

3. Storage: Store in a sealed container and use within 2 months.

Digestive Health Recipes:

1. Preparation:

   o Mix castor oil with lemon juice or other digestive aids according to the recipe.

2. Application:

   o For constipation relief, take the mixture orally, as directed (usually small doses such as 1 tsp of castor oil combined with juice).

   o Ensure you consult with a healthcare provider before using castor oil for digestive purposes.

3. Storage: Keep in the refrigerator and consume within a week.

Foot and Hand Care Recipes:

1. Preparation:

   o Combine castor oil with ingredients like shea butter or coconut oil.

   o Stir until the consistency is smooth.

2. Application:

   o Massage the mixture into dry or cracked areas of the feet or hands.

   o For cracked heels, apply at night and wear socks to allow the mixture to absorb overnight.

3. Storage: Store in an airtight container for up to 3 months.

Detox and Cleansing Recipes:

1. Preparation:

   o Blend castor oil with detoxifying essential oils such as tea tree or peppermint oil.

   o Mix until all components are well incorporated.

2. Application:

   o For detoxifying foot soaks or body scrubs, apply to the skin, rub gently, and leave on for about 20 minutes before rinsing.

3. Storage: Store in a cool, dark place for up to 1 month.

Recipes

Skin Healing and Moisturizing

Castor Oil for Dry Skin:

o 1 tbsp castor oil

o 1 tbsp jojoba oil (moisturizing)

o 3 drops rose essential oil (soothing and fragrant)

Usage: Apply a thin layer to dry areas before bed.

Castor Oil Night Moisturizer:

o 1 tbsp castor oil

o 1 tsp almond oil (nourishing)

o 2 drops lavender essential oil (calming)

Usage: Apply before bed.

Sunburn Relief:

o 2 tbsp castor oil

o 1 tbsp aloe vera gel (cooling and healing)

o 3 drops chamomile essential oil (anti-inflammatory)

Healing Cracked Heels:

o 1 tbsp castor oil

o 1 tbsp coconut oil (moisturizing and antimicrobial)

o 2 drops tea tree essential oil (antifungal)

Usage: Rub castor oil on cracked heels and wear socks overnight.

Anti-Aging Serum:

o 1 tbsp castor oil

o 1 tsp rosehip seed oil (regenerating)

o 2 drops frankincense essential oil (anti-aging)

Eczema Relief:

o 1 tbsp castor oil

o 1 tbsp shea butter (hydrating and soothing)

o 2 drops chamomile essential oil (anti-inflammatory)

Psoriasis Treatment:

- 1 tbsp castor oil

- 1 tsp avocado oil (nourishing)

- 2 drops calendula essential oil (healing)

Scar Reduction:

- 1 tbsp castor oil

- 1 tsp rosehip oil (skin regeneration)

- 3 drops helichrysum essential oil (promotes healing)

Usage: Massage castor oil into scars twice daily to help fade them.

Stretch Mark Prevention:

- 2 tbsp castor oil

- 1 tbsp cocoa butter (moisturizing)

- 3 drops lavender essential oil (skin repair)

Usage: Apply castor oil to the belly during pregnancy.

Dry Lip Balm:

- 1 tbsp castor oil

- 1 tsp beeswax (seals in moisture)

- 2 drops peppermint essential oil (soothing)

Usage: Mix castor oil with beeswax and apply to lips for hydration.

Hair Growth and Scalp Health

Castor Oil Hair Mask:

- 2 tbsp castor oil

- 1 tbsp coconut oil (deep conditioning)

- 5 drops rosemary essential oil (stimulates growth)

Usage: Massage into scalp, leave overnight, and wash out in the morning.

Anti-Dandruff Treatment:

- 1 tbsp castor oil

- 1 tbsp olive oil (soothing)

- 5 drops tea tree essential oil (antifungal)

Split Ends Repair:

- 1 tbsp castor oil

- 1 tsp argan oil (restorative)

- 3 drops ylang-ylang essential oil (hair strength)

Usage: Apply castor oil to split ends and leave for an hour before washing.

Hair Growth Booster:

- 1 tbsp castor oil

- 1 tbsp peppermint oil (stimulates circulation)

- 1 tsp coconut oil (nourishing)

Deep Conditioning Treatment:

- 2 tbsp castor oil

- 1 tbsp shea butter (moisturizing)

- 2 drops lavender essential oil (calming)

Usage: Mix castor oil with coconut oil and leave on hair for 2 hours.

Eyebrow Growth Serum:

- 1 tsp castor oil

- 1 tsp argan oil (nourishing)

- 2 drops rosemary essential oil (growth-stimulating)

Usage: Apply castor oil to eyebrows using a clean brush.

Eyelash Growth Serum:

- 1 tsp castor oil

- 1 tsp vitamin E oil (strengthening)

- 2 drops lavender essential oil (nourishing)

Usage: Apply castor oil to eyelashes before bed for fuller lashes.

Thicker Beard Oil:

- 1 tbsp castor oil

- 1 tsp jojoba oil (moisturizing)

- 3 drops cedarwood essential oil (hair growth)

Hair Loss Prevention:

- 1 tbsp castor oil

- 1 tbsp black seed oil (anti-inflammatory)

- 5 drops rosemary essential oil (stimulating growth)

Frizz Control Serum:

- 1 tsp castor oil

- 1 tsp argan oil (smoothing)

- 2 drops lavender essential oil (calming scent)

Joint and Muscle Pain Relief

Castor Oil Pack for Joint Pain:

- 1 tbsp castor oil

- 1 tsp ginger essential oil (anti-inflammatory)

- 1 tsp turmeric powder (pain relief)

Usage: Soak a cloth in castor oil, place on the joint, and cover with a heating pad.

Arthritis Pain Relief:

- 1 tbsp castor oil

- 1 tsp cayenne pepper oil (stimulates blood flow)

- 2 drops eucalyptus essential oil (pain relief)

Muscle Pain Relief:

- 1 tbsp castor oil

- 1 tsp magnesium oil (muscle relaxation)

- 3 drops peppermint essential oil (cooling effect)

Back Pain Relief:

- 1 tbsp castor oil

- 1 tsp arnica oil (pain-relieving)

- 2 drops clove essential oil (anti-inflammatory)

Usage: Apply castor oil directly to the lower back and cover with a heating pad.

Sore Feet Treatment:

- 1 tbsp castor oil

- 1 tsp menthol crystals (soothing)

- 3 drops peppermint essential oil (cooling)

Usage: Rub castor oil on sore feet and massage for 5 minutes.

Knee Pain Pack:

- 1 tbsp castor oil

- 1 tsp turmeric essential oil (anti-inflammatory)

- 2 drops ginger essential oil (pain relief)

Usage: Soak a cloth in castor oil, wrap around the knee, and leave for an hour.

Castor Oil for Tendonitis:

- 1 tbsp castor oil

- 1 tsp arnica oil (pain relief)

- 2 drops marjoram essential oil (soothing)

Frozen Shoulder Treatment:

- 1 tbsp castor oil

- 1 tsp wintergreen oil (pain-relieving)

- 2 drops lavender essential oil (calming)

Carpal Tunnel Relief:

- 1 tbsp castor oil
- 1 tsp frankincense oil (anti-inflammatory)
- 2 drops peppermint essential oil (cooling)

Usage: Massage castor oil into wrists and cover with a warm cloth.

Tennis Elbow Treatment:

- 1 tbsp castor oil
- 1 tsp cayenne oil (stimulates circulation)
- 2 drops eucalyptus essential oil (pain relief)

Digestive and Internal Health

Castor Oil Laxative:

- 1 tbsp castor oil
- 1 tsp lemon juice (improves taste)
- 1 tsp honey (sweetens and soothes)

Usage: Take 1-2 teaspoons of castor oil to relieve constipation.

Castor Oil Belly Massage:

- 1 tbsp castor oil
- 1 tsp coconut oil (hydrating)
- 2 drops ginger essential oil (aids digestion)

Usage: Massage the abdomen with castor oil for digestive issues.

Castor Oil Detox Pack:

- 1 tbsp castor oil
- 1 tsp eucalyptus oil (stimulates detox)
- 1 tsp lavender essential oil (calming)

Usage: Apply castor oil to the abdomen and cover with a warm cloth for liver detoxification.

Gallbladder Cleanse:

- 1 tbsp castor oil
- 1 tsp apple cider vinegar (boosts cleansing)
- 1 tsp lemon juice (detoxifying)

Usage: Mix castor oil with lemon juice and drink to cleanse the gallbladder.

Bloating Relief:

- 1 tbsp castor oil

- 1 tsp fennel oil (reduces bloating)

- 2 drops peppermint oil (soothing)

Usage: Massage castor oil into the stomach to reduce bloating.

Hemorrhoid Relief:

- 1 tbsp castor oil

- 1 tsp witch hazel (soothing)

- 2 drops cypress essential oil (anti-inflammatory)

Irritable Bowel Syndrome (IBS) Relief Pack:

- 1 tbsp castor oil

- 1 tsp ginger essential oil (anti-inflammatory)

- 2 drops chamomile essential oil (soothing)

Usage: Place a castor oil pack on the stomach to alleviate symptoms of IBS.

Liver Detox:

- 1 tbsp castor oil

- 1 tsp lemon essential oil (detoxifying)

- 1 tsp rosemary essential oil (stimulates detox)

Usage: Apply castor oil pack over the liver for detoxification.

Colon Cleanse:

- 1 tbsp castor oil

- 1 tsp aloe vera juice (cleansing)

- 1 tsp lemon juice (detoxifying)

Gastric Ulcer Treatment:

- 1 tbsp castor oil

- 1 tsp aloe vera gel (soothing)

- 2 drops chamomile essential oil (anti-inflammatory)

Usage: Massage castor oil on the abdomen to reduce symptoms.

Skin Conditions and Blemishes

Acne Treatment:

- 1 tsp castor oil

- 1 tsp witch hazel (antibacterial)

- 2 drops tea tree essential oil (acne-fighting)

Usage: Dab castor oil on blemishes and leave overnight.

Castor Oil for Blackheads:

- 1 tsp castor oil

- 1 tsp jojoba oil (balancing)

- 2 drops lavender essential oil (calming)

Usage: Apply castor oil to blackheads and massage in circular motions.

Boil Treatment:

- 1 tsp castor oil

- 1 tsp turmeric powder (anti-inflammatory)

- 2 drops tea tree essential oil (antibacterial)

Usage: Apply castor oil to boils to help drain and heal them.

Fungal Infection Treatment:

- 1 tsp castor oil

- 1 tsp coconut oil (antifungal)

- 2 drops oregano essential oil (antifungal)

Wart Removal:

- 1 tsp castor oil

- 1 tsp apple cider vinegar (helps dissolve warts)

- 2 drops tea tree essential oil (antiviral)

Usage: Apply castor oil directly to the wart daily until it disappears.

Rosacea Treatment:

- 1 tsp castor oil

- 1 tsp argan oil (soothing)

- 2 drops chamomile essential oil (anti-inflammatory)

Cold Sore Treatment:

- 1 tsp castor oil

- 1 tsp coconut oil (antiviral)

- 2 drops tea tree essential oil (antiviral)

Sunspot Removal:

- 1 tsp castor oil

- 1 tsp lemon juice (lightens spots)

- 2 drops frankincense essential oil (promotes even skin tone)

Shingles Relief:

- 1 tbsp castor oil

- 1 tsp aloe vera gel (soothing)

- 2 drops eucalyptus essential oil (pain relief)

Bruise Healing:

- 1 tsp castor oil

- 1 tsp arnica oil (reduces bruising)

- 2 drops lavender essential oil (calming)

Anti-Inflammatory and Pain Relief

Arthritis Balm:

- 1 tbsp castor oil

- 1 tbsp shea butter (soothing)

- 3 drops ginger essential oil (anti-inflammatory)

Sciatica Pain Relief:

- 1 tbsp castor oil

- 1 tsp arnica oil (pain relief)

- 3 drops peppermint essential oil (cooling effect)

Tendonitis Soother:

- 1 tbsp castor oil

- 1 tsp calendula oil (healing)

- 2 drops eucalyptus essential oil (pain relief)

Neck Pain Massage Oil:

- 1 tbsp castor oil

- 1 tsp grapeseed oil (light texture)

- 2 drops lavender essential oil (calming)

Plantar Fasciitis Relief:

- 1 tbsp castor oil

- 1 tsp peppermint oil (soothing)

- 1 tsp arnica oil (anti-inflammatory)

Joint Inflammation Balm:

- 1 tbsp castor oil

- 1 tsp turmeric oil (anti-inflammatory)

- 2 drops frankincense essential oil (healing)

Swelling Reduction:

- 1 tbsp castor oil

- 1 tsp black seed oil (anti-inflammatory)

- 2 drops ginger essential oil (stimulates circulation)

Rheumatoid Arthritis Relief:

- 1 tbsp castor oil

- 1 tsp evening primrose oil (anti-inflammatory)

- 2 drops rosemary essential oil (pain relief)

Sports Injury Healing Balm:

- 1 tbsp castor oil

- 1 tsp comfrey oil (healing)

- 2 drops peppermint essential oil (pain relief)

Bruised Rib Treatment:

- 1 tbsp castor oil

- 1 tsp turmeric oil (pain relief)

- 2 drops lavender essential oil (soothing)

Respiratory Health

Cough and Cold Chest Rub:

- 1 tbsp castor oil

- 1 tsp eucalyptus oil (decongestant)

- 2 drops peppermint essential oil (soothing)

Usage: Rub castor oil on the chest and back to ease a cough.

Sinus Infection Relief:

- 1 tbsp castor oil

- 1 tsp tea tree oil (antibacterial)

- 2 drops eucalyptus essential oil (clears sinuses)

Usage: Massage castor oil onto the chest and neck to reduce congestion.

Congestion Relief:

- 1 tbsp castor oil

- 1 tsp eucalyptus oil (decongestant)

- 2 drops peppermint essential oil (soothing)

Asthma Symptom Relief:

- 1 tbsp castor oil

- 1 tsp black seed oil (anti-inflammatory)

- 2 drops lavender essential oil (calming)

Usage: Massage castor oil on the chest to ease asthma symptoms.

Bronchitis Treatment:

- 1 tbsp castor oil

- 1 tsp thyme essential oil (antibacterial)

- 2 drops eucalyptus essential oil (decongestant)

Usage: Rub castor oil on the chest to help open airways.

Chest Congestion Rub:

- 1 tbsp castor oil

- 1 tsp coconut oil (hydrating)

- 2 drops camphor essential oil (expectorant)

Allergy Relief:

- 1 tbsp castor oil

- 1 tsp peppermint oil (calms inflammation)

- 2 drops eucalyptus essential oil (soothes breathing)

Usage: Rub castor oil on the chest to reduce allergic reactions.

Seasonal Allergy Balm:

- 1 tbsp castor oil

- 1 tsp calendula oil (soothing)

- 2 drops chamomile essential oil (calming)

Cold Sore Respiratory Relief:

- 1 tbsp castor oil

- 1 tsp lemon essential oil (clears sinuses)

- 2 drops rosemary essential oil (decongestant)

Wheezing Symptom Balm:

- 1 tbsp castor oil

- 1 tsp oregano oil (antiviral)

- 2 drops lavender essential oil (calming)

Oral and Dental Health

Toothache Remedy:

- 1 tsp castor oil

- 1 tsp clove oil (pain relief)

- 1 drop peppermint oil (antiseptic)

Gum Infection Treatment:

- 1 tsp castor oil

- 1 tsp tea tree oil (antibacterial)

- 2 drops myrrh essential oil (healing)

Mouth Ulcer Relief:

- 1 tsp castor oil

- 1 tsp aloe vera gel (soothing)

- 2 drops tea tree essential oil (antibacterial)

Usage: Dab castor oil on mouth ulcers to soothe and heal.

Teeth Whitening Solution:

- 1 tsp castor oil
- 1 tsp baking soda (removes stains)
- 2 drops peppermint oil (freshens breath)

Oral Thrush Treatment:

- 1 tsp castor oil
- 1 tsp coconut oil (antifungal)
- 2 drops clove essential oil (antimicrobial)

Bleeding Gums Relief:

- 1 tsp castor oil
- 1 tsp witch hazel (astringent)
- 2 drops myrrh essential oil (soothing)

Bad Breath Cure:

- 1 tsp castor oil
- 1 tsp peppermint oil (freshens breath)
- 1 drop clove essential oil (antibacterial)

Canker Sore Treatment:

- 1 tsp castor oil

- 1 tsp calendula oil (healing)
- 1 drop tea tree essential oil (antibacterial)

Jaw Pain Relief:

- 1 tsp castor oil
- 1 tsp arnica oil (pain relief)
- 2 drops lavender essential oil (calming)

Sore Throat Remedy:

- 1 tsp castor oil
- 1 tsp honey (soothing)
- 1 drop lemon essential oil (antibacterial)

Immune and Detox Support

Immune-Boosting Rub:

- 1 tbsp castor oil
- 1 tsp oregano oil (antiviral)
- 2 drops eucalyptus essential oil (boosts immune system)

Usage: Rub castor oil on the chest and abdomen to stimulate the immune system.

Detoxifying Massage Oil:

- 1 tbsp castor oil

- 1 tsp rosemary essential oil (stimulates detox)

- 1 tsp lemon essential oil (detoxifying)

Lymphatic Drainage Massage:

- 1 tbsp castor oil

- 1 tsp frankincense essential oil (stimulates lymph flow)

- 1 tsp ginger essential oil (detoxifying)

Usage: Massage castor oil into lymph nodes to stimulate drainage.

Fever Reduction Pack:

- 1 tbsp castor oil

- 1 tsp peppermint oil (cooling effect)

- 1 tsp eucalyptus essential oil (lowers fever)

Usage: Apply castor oil packs to the abdomen to help reduce fever.

Liver Detoxification:

- 1 tbsp castor oil

- 1 tsp lemon juice (cleansing)

- 1 tsp rosemary essential oil (supports liver function)

Spleen Health Support:

- 1 tbsp castor oil

- 1 tsp black seed oil (detoxifying)

- 1 tsp lemon essential oil (supports spleen health)

Colon Detox Massage Oil:

- 1 tbsp castor oil

- 1 tsp aloe vera juice (cleansing)

- 2 drops ginger essential oil (stimulates digestion)

Immune System Booster:

- 1 tbsp castor oil

- 1 tsp thyme essential oil (immune-boosting)

- 1 tsp oregano essential oil (antiviral)

Cold and Flu Balm:

- 1 tbsp castor oil

- 1 tsp eucalyptus oil (decongestant)

- 2 drops thyme essential oil (antiviral)

Kidney Detox Massage:

- 1 tbsp castor oil
- 1 tsp juniper essential oil (supports kidney function)
- 1 tsp lemon essential oil (detoxifying)

Overall Wellness and Body Care

Anti-Bacterial Cleanser:

- 1 tsp castor oil
- 1 tsp witch hazel (antibacterial)
- 2 drops tea tree essential oil (antiseptic)

Sleep Aid Balm:

- 1 tbsp castor oil
- 1 tsp lavender essential oil (calming)
- 2 drops chamomile essential oil (soothing)

Energy Booster:

- 1 tsp castor oil
- 1 tsp peppermint essential oil (stimulates energy)
- 1 tsp rosemary essential oil (boosts focus)

Improved Circulation Massage:

- 1 tbsp castor oil
- 1 tsp ginger essential oil (stimulates circulation)
- 1 tsp cypress essential oil (promotes blood flow)

Detoxifying Foot Rub:

- 1 tbsp castor oil
- 1 tsp tea tree oil (detoxifying)
- 2 drops peppermint essential oil (stimulates circulation)

Stretch Mark Prevention:

- 1 tbsp castor oil
- 1 tsp rosehip oil (healing)
- 2 drops lavender essential oil (soothing)

Wrinkle-Reducing Serum:

- 1 tsp castor oil
- 1 tsp argan oil (anti-aging)
- 2 drops rose essential oil (moisturizing)

Restorative Hand Cream:

- 1 tbsp castor oil

- 1 tsp shea butter (moisturizing)

- 2 drops lavender essential oil (calming)

Nail Strengthening Serum:

- 1 tsp castor oil

- 1 tsp jojoba oil (strengthening)

- 2 drops rosemary essential oil (nourishing)

Eco-Friendly Household Uses of Castor Oil.

In an ever more environmentally conscious world, more and more people are looking for sustainable alternatives to regular products. Traditional household cleaning supplies are frequently loaded with harsh chemicals that can harm both the environment and human health.

Castor oil is a practical and environmentally beneficial option for a variety of home duties. Aside from its incredible skin, hair, and health benefits, it can be a powerful partner in creating a greener, chemical-free household.

This chapter discusses creative methods to use castor oil for environmentally friendly household cleaning and maintenance.
By including castor oil into your regular cleaning and home care routines, you may help lessen your environmental impact while keeping a healthy and clean-living environment.

Why is Castor Oil an Eco-Friendly Household Solution?

Castor oil's environmental benefits stem from its natural plant roots. Castor oil, extracted from the seeds of the Ricinus communis plant, is biodegradable[28], non-toxic[29], and free of synthetic compounds. Unlike many conventional cleaning solutions, which release toxic chemicals into the air and water, is a mild, long-lasting alternative for a variety of home activities.

28 (Patel, 2016)
29 (Swenson P. S., The antimicrobial activity of castor oil and its relation to ricinoleic acid content. , 1990)

Its high fatty acid content, lends it unique qualities that make it a good cleaning, polishing, and pest control agent. It functions as a natural disinfectant30, degreaser, and lubricant31 in one substance. This adaptability means that a single bottle of castor oil can replace several chemical-based cleaners, decreasing waste and the quantity of dangerous substances in your home.

Safe for you and the environment.

One of the most significant benefits of utilizing castor oil for domestic uses is that it is safe for you, your family, and the environment. Unlike traditional cleaning chemicals, which frequently contain volatile organic compounds (VOCs) and other dangerous substances, castor oil is non-toxic and does not add to indoor air pollution. This makes it a perfect alternative for households with children, pets, or those who are chemically sensitive.

Also, because castor oil is biodegradable, washing it down the drain will not affect waterways or ecosystems, making it an environmentally responsible choice for consumers. Whether you use it as a cleaning agent, a natural polish, or a pest repellent, castor oil is a safe and effective option that will not harm your home or the environment.

Simplifying Your Homecare Routine

Incorporating castor oil into your household routine is a simple yet effective approach to streamline your home care products. By replacing a range of specialist cleaning solutions with a single multi-purpose, natural oil, you eliminate clutter and simplify your cleaning process.

---

30 (Vieira C. E., Ricinoleic acid, a specific agonist of capsaicin receptor, induces hyperalgesia in guinea-pigs., 2002)
31 (O'Dell, 2018)

Furthermore, castor oil is easily blended with other natural products such as baking soda, vinegar, and essential oils, allowing you to create personalized, eco-friendly remedies for every part of your home.

Castor oil can degrease surfaces, repel insects[32], and restore the gloss to your wooden furniture—all while remaining safe, effective, and environmentally friendly

.

Recipes

Here are 30 creative, eco-friendly castor oil recipes for household cleaning and other solutions, along with their usage instructions:

All-Purpose Cleaner

- 1 cup water
- 1/4 cup white vinegar
- 1 tablespoon castor oil
- 10 drops essential oil

Usage: Mix all ingredients in a spray bottle. Spray on surfaces like countertops, sinks, and tiles, then wipe with a clean cloth.

Furniture Polish
        2 tablespoons castor oil
        1/4 cup olive oil
        1 tablespoon lemon juice
Usage: Apply a small amount to a soft cloth and rub gently into wooden furniture. Buff with a clean, dry cloth to bring out the shine.

Stain Remover
        1 tablespoon castor oil
        1 teaspoon baking soda
        2 tablespoons water
Usage: Apply the paste to fabric stains, rub gently, let it sit for 15-30 minutes, then wash as usual.

Natural Soap Making
        1 cup castor oil
        2 cups olive oil
        1/2 cup coconut oil
        4 oz melt-and-pour soap base
        1 cup water
Usage: Combine the oils. Mix the soap base with water (carefully), then combine with the oils. Stir until thick, then pour into molds. Let sit for 24-48 hours before using as natural soap.

Stainless Steel Cleaner

        1/4 cup castor oil
        1/4 cup white vinegar
        5 drops lemon essential oil
    Usage:

---

32 (Broglie, 2015)

Apply to a microfiber cloth and rub onto stainless steel appliances to remove smudges. Buff for a streak-free finish.

6. Leather Conditioner

2 tablespoons castor oil
1 tablespoon coconut oil
Usage:
Apply to leather items with a cloth, massaging gently. Let it absorb for 30 minutes, then buff with a clean cloth.

7. Wood Floor Polish

1/4 cup castor oil
1/4 cup white vinegar
1 cup water
Usage:
Mix in a spray bottle. Lightly spray onto wood floors and mop. Let dry for a shiny finish.

8. Natural Degreaser

1 tablespoon castor oil
2 tablespoons baking soda
2 cups warm water
Usage:
Mix ingredients and apply to greasy surfaces (like stove tops). Let it sit for 5-10 minutes, then scrub and wipe clean.

9. Bug Repellent Spray

1 tablespoon castor oil

10 drops eucalyptus essential oil
1 cup water
Usage:
Shake well and spray around doors, windows, or outdoor areas to repel insects.

10. Rust Prevention

1 tablespoon castor oil
1 tablespoon olive oil
Usage:
Rub onto metal tools or surfaces with a cloth to prevent rust and corrosion. Reapply every few months as needed.

11. Eco-Friendly Paint Remover

2 tablespoons castor oil
1 tablespoon lemon juice
Usage:
Apply to old paint spots and let it sit for 15-30 minutes. Scrape away softened paint.

12. Natural Carpet Cleaner

2 tablespoons castor oil
1/4 cup baking soda
10 drops essential oil (optional)
Usage:
Sprinkle the mixture over carpets. Let it sit for 10 minutes, then vacuum. Ideal for removing stains and odors.

13. Squeaky Door Fix

Pure castor oil (as needed)
Usage:
Apply a few drops to squeaky hinges or locks. Open and close the door to distribute the oil evenly.

Candle Wax Remover

1 tablespoon castor oil
1 tablespoon white vinegar

Usage:Dab the mixture on wax spills and let it sit for 5-10 minutes. Gently scrape away the softened wax.

15. Pet-Safe Flea Spray

2 tablespoons castor oil
1 cup water
10 drops lavender essential oil
Usage:
Shake well and spray on pet bedding or carpets to repel fleas naturally. Avoid direct application to pets.

16. Glass Cleaner

1/4 cup castor oil
1/2 cup white vinegar
1 cup water
Usage:
Spray onto glass surfaces, then wipe with a clean, dry cloth for streak-free windows and mirrors.

17. Eco-Friendly Laundry Booster

1 tablespoon castor oil

1/2 cup baking soda
Usage:
Add to your washing machine to help remove stains and naturally soften fabrics.

18. Non-Toxic Candle Making

1/2 cup castor oil
1/2 cup beeswax
Essential oil (optional)
Usage:
Melt the beeswax, mix with castor oil, and add essential oil if desired. Pour into molds and let harden for a clean-burning candle.

19. Natural Silver Polish

1 tablespoon castor oil
1 tablespoon baking soda
Usage:
Mix into a paste and apply to tarnished silver. Rub gently with a soft cloth, then rinse and dry.

20. Mold and Mildew Prevention

2 tablespoons castor oil
1 tablespoon tea tree essential oil
1 cup water
Usage:
Spray on areas prone to mold and mildew (bathrooms, basements). Wipe off after letting it sit for 10 minutes.

21. Bathtub and Tile Cleaner

2 tablespoons castor oil

1/4 cup baking soda

10 drops eucalyptus oil

Usage:

Scrub onto tubs and tiles to remove soap scum and disinfect. Rinse thoroughly.

Eco-Friendly Dusting Spray

1 tablespoon castor oil

1 cup water

5 drops lemon essential oil

Usage:Lightly mist onto surfaces, then wipe with a clean cloth to pick up dust and add shine.

Natural Fabric Freshener

1 tablespoon castor oil

1 cup water

10 drops essential oil (optional)

Usage:

Spray onto curtains, cushions, or linens for a refreshing, natural scent.

24. Drain Cleaner

1 tablespoon castor oil

1/2 cup baking soda

1/2 cup vinegar

Usage:

Pour the baking soda and vinegar into the drain, followed by the castor oil. Let it fizz, then flush with hot water after 10 minutes.

25. Oven Cleaner

2 tablespoons castor oil

1/4 cup baking soda

1/4 cup white vinegar

Usage:

Apply the paste to oven surfaces and let it sit for 15 minutes. Scrub away grease and residue, then rinse.

26. Grease Trap Cleaner

2 tablespoons castor oil

1/4 cup baking soda

1/4 cup hot water

Usage:

Pour into grease traps to help break down buildup and prevent clogs.

27. Eco-Friendly Deodorizer

1 tablespoon castor oil

1/4 cup baking soda

10 drops essential oil

Usage:

Sprinkle the mixture into shoes, closets, or refrigerators to absorb odors.

Wallpaper Removal Solution

2 tablespoons castor oil

1/2 cup white vinegar

1 cup water

Usage:

Spray onto wallpaper adhesive and let it sit for 15 minutes. Peel off the softened wallpaper with ease.

29. Non-Toxic Air Freshener

1 tablespoon castor oil

1 cup water

10 drops essential oil (your choice)

Usage:

Mist into the air to refresh the room without chemicals.

Natural Tarnish Remover

1 tablespoon castor oil

1 tablespoon lemon juice

Usage:

Apply to tarnished metal surfaces, rub gently, then wipe clean for a renewed shine.

Figure 1: Ricinus Comunis Seeds

The Ricinus Plant and the Production of Castor Oil

Castor oil, known for its numerous healing and wellness benefits, is derived from the seeds of the *Ricinus communis* plant. Understanding the origins of this extraordinary oil enhances its historical relevance and present applications. In this chapter, we'll look at the history of the ricinus plant, its biological makeup, and how castor oil is harvested to maintain its beneficial features.

The Ricinus Plant: Natural Source of Castor Oil

Ricinus communis, sometimes known as the castor plant, is a sturdy and resistant plant found in tropical Africa and India. Over the years, it has spread throughout the world, thriving in warm regions. While castor oil is derived from its seeds, the plant as a whole is remarkable in terms of botany and agriculture.

Botanical characteristics of the Ricinus plant include its size and structure. Under ideal conditions, the ricinus plant can reach heights of up to 12 feet (3.6 meters). Its big, glossy, and lobed leaves lend it a distinct tropical aspect.

The plant produces green to reddish flower clusters and seeds. After pollination, the plant produces spiny seed pods that contain the seeds used to make castor oil.

Seed Toxicity: Despite producing useful oil, the seeds contain ricin, a deadly poison. Ricin is one of the most toxic compounds found in nature, and even little doses can be lethal. However, during the oil extraction process, ricin is securely removed, making the oil safe to use.

The ricinus plant's flexibility allows it to thrive in a wide range of conditions, making it a sustainable source of oil in many regions of the world. Today, India is the world's largest producer of castor oil, accounting for more than 85% of total production.

From Seed to Oil: The Castor Oil Extraction Process

Castor oil production is a sophisticated procedure that ensures the elimination of dangerous chemicals such as ricin while maintaining the oil's therapeutic characteristics. The process used to extract the oil has a considerable impact on its quality, purity, and potency. There are two types of extraction: cold pressing and solvent extraction.

Harvest the Seeds

Ricinus communis plants yield ripe seed pods, which are harvested and the seeds removed from the pods. Each seed has a substantial amount of oil, accounting for around 30-50% of its bulk.

The appearance of the seeds: The seeds are oval-shaped and have a distinctive mottled look of brown, gray, and black.

Raw seeds contain ricin, which is a highly dangerous chemical. The extraction procedure is intended to eliminate ricin, guaranteeing that the oil is safe for food and topical use.

Cold Pressing Method

Cold-pressing is the most traditional and recommended process for producing high-quality castor oil. Mechanically pressing the seeds without using heat preserves the oil's natural nutrients and beneficial characteristics.

How it works: The seeds are cleaned and dried before being fed through a mechanical press. This press applies substantial pressure, extracting the oil without the need for high heat. Cold-pressing preserves the oil's high concentration of ricinoleic acid, which is primarily responsible for its anti-inflammatory and therapeutic qualities.

Cold-pressed castor oil is considered best since it maintains its potent qualities. It remains devoid of chemical residues and has a higher nutritional value.

Cold-pressing produces a golden yellow oil with a slightly thick, viscous viscosity.

Solvent Extraction Method.

While cold-pressing is the preferred method for high-quality castor oil, some commercial production facilities use solvent extraction to produce more oil. This method extracts oil from seeds using a solvent (usually hexane).

How It Works: The seeds are first ground into a fine powder and then combined with the solvent. The solvent helps to dissolve the oil, which is subsequently separated from the seed residue.

After extraction, the oil is refined to eliminate contaminants and residual solvents. The final product is filtered and treated to remove poisons such as ricin.

Solvent-extracted castor oil is lighter in color compared to cold-pressed oil. This approach, however, is less popular for personal care and pharmaceutical applications due to the possibility of chemical residues from the solvent.

Removing Ricin and Purify the Oil

Regardless of the extraction method used, one of the most important steps in generating castor oil is the elimination of ricin. During the pressing or solvent extraction process, ricin is rendered inactive and eliminated from the finished product, making it safe for eating and topical use. This guarantees that castor oil can be utilized without causing any adverse effects.

Packaging and Distribution.

Once cleansed and filtered, the oil is packaged in glass or plastic bottles and ready for distribution. Cold-pressed castor oil is frequently marketed as "organic" or "pure" due to its minimum processing, whereas solvent-extracted oils may be classified as "refined."

Types of Castor Oil: Cold-pressed versus Jamaican Black Castor Oil.

Castor oil comes in several different kinds, each with its own set of qualities and applications. The two most common types are cold-pressed castor oil and Jamaican black castor oil.

Cold-Pressed Castor Oil: Produced by pressing seeds without heat or chemicals. It's golden yellow in color and slightly thicker in substance. Because of its purity and high nutrient content, cold-pressed castor oil is excellent for skincare, hair care, and medical applications.

Jamaican Black Castor Oil is prepared differently by roasting the seeds before pressing them. The ash from the roasted seeds gives the oil a characteristic dark hue and a stronger scent. Jamaican black castor oil is very famous for stimulating hair development and scalp health because the roasting process improves its capacity to increase circulation and nourish hair follicles.

When purchasing castor oil, it is important to look into the extraction method and the desired application. Here are some recommendations for choosing the proper product:

Only use pharmaceutical-grade castor oil for internal or therapeutic uses. These oils have been specifically refined and verified for safety.

Sustainability of Castor Oil Production

Castor oil production is often seen as environmentally friendly because the ricinus plant is drought-tolerant and can be produced in desert locations where other crops struggle to thrive. Furthermore, the entire seed is employed in the oil extraction process, which reduces waste. However, sustainability is also dependent on ethical sourcing and fair trading procedures, especially in nations where castor oil is a significant agricultural export.

Conclusion: From nature to wellness.

Castor oil's journey from the seeds of the Ricinus communis plant to the bottles on our stores demonstrates its long-term usefulness and adaptability. The extraction procedures used to create this exceptional oil highlight not only the necessity of maintaining its natural nutrients, but also the care required to ensure its safety and efficacy for a wide range of applications.

Whether used for skincare, hair care, or medicine, castor oil remains one of the most powerful and versatile oils available, with a history as rich as its therapeutic properties. As you continue to learn about its numerous benefits in the following chapters, keep in mind that the simple yet effective method that produces castor oil is what makes it such a powerful weapon for natural wellbeing.

Finding Quality Castor Oil Products

Castor oil is a versatile ingredient, however, not all products are created equally. The quality of castor oil varies significantly, and using a low-grade product could lower its efficiency while also introducing unwanted chemicals or contaminants into your body.

This chapter will help you navigate the castor oil market by providing practical recommendations for identifying high-quality goods, avoiding low-quality or adulterated oils, and ensuring you get the most out of this potent natural medicine.

Why Quality Matters: A Comparison of High and Low-Quality Oil

The method of extracting, refining, and storing castor oil has a significant impact on its quality. High-quality oil preserves its rich nutritional profile and is devoid of contaminants and additions, whereas low-quality goods may be diluted, chemically treated, or polluted with impurities. These elements have a direct impact on the oil's effectiveness and, in certain situations, may be harmful if the product contains chemicals or irritants.

High-Quality Castor Oil maintains its high concentration of ricinoleic acid, is devoid of hazardous compounds, and is treated without compromising its nutritional value.

Low-Quality Oil on the other hand, may be diluted with other oils, treated with chemicals, or contaminated with impurities decreasing its effectiveness and safety.

Tips for Choosing High-Quality Castor Oil Products while Avoiding Low-Quality or Potentially Harmful Options

Look for Cold Pressed Castor Oil.

The process used to extract castor oil is a key aspect in determining its quality. Cold-pressed castor oil is regarded the greatest quality since it is produced from castor seeds without the use of heat or chemicals, keeping the oil's inherent nutrients and therapeutic characteristics.

Why This Matters: Cold-pressing is the process of extracting oil from castor seeds at low temperatures. This process preserves the oil's beneficial components, including ricinoleic acid, vital fatty acids, and vitamins. In contrast, oils extracted with heat or chemical solvents may lose some of their nutrients and include trace amounts of hazardous substances.

Check the label for words like "*cold-pressed*" or "*expeller-pressed.*" These results demonstrate that the oil was extracted naturally, without the application of heat or chemical solvents. Cold-pressed castor oil typically has a thicker viscosity and a deep golden tint.

Select organic and certified products.

When looking for high-quality castor oil, another important element to consider is organic certification. Organic castor oil is made without synthetic fertilizers, pesticides, or genetically modified organisms (GMOs), making it a safer and more environmentally friendly option.

Why This Matters: Non-organic castor oil may be obtained from castor seeds that were treated with synthetic agents during cultivation. These compounds may leave residues in the oil, causing skin irritation or diminishing its purity. Institutions certify organic products, ensuring that the oil is produced in accordance with strict agricultural and processing standards.

What to Look For: Look for organic certification marks from respected organizations like USDA Organic, ECOCERT, and the Soil Association Organic. These certifications ensure that the oil was produced without using harmful chemicals and was examined to fulfill organic farming standards.

Check for Hexane-Free Castor Oil.

Hexane is a chemical solvent commonly used in the extraction of several oils, including castor oil. While this approach is less expensive and produces more oil, hexane can leave potentially harmful residue that are could be dangerous to your health.

Why This Matters: Hexane-extracted oils may contain trace levels of this chemical, which can cause skin irritation and other health problems if used frequently. Furthermore, the use of hexane in the extraction process might deplete the oil's essential elements, lowering its efficiency.

When purchasing castor oil, make sure the label clearly indicates "hexane-free." This means that the oil was not extracted using chemical solvents and is suitable for daily usage, particularly for skincare or internal intake.

Check the label for additives and fillers.

Pure castor oil should have only one ingredient: castor oil. Some lower-quality goods may be diluted with other oils or contain additives such as preservatives, scents, or synthetic chemicals, reducing the oil's effectiveness and causing discomfort, especially on sensitive skin.

Why It Matters: Additives and fillers can compromise the purity of castor oil, resulting in allergic responses or closed pores when applied to the skin. Products containing scents or preservatives can potentially damage the oil's natural therapeutic capabilities.

What to Look For: Carefully read the ingredient label. High-quality castor oil should contain only one ingredient: Ricinus communis (castor oil). If you notice any other components, such as aroma, preservatives, or other oils, try purchasing a different product to guarantee you are getting pure castor oil.

Look for dark glass bottles.

Another factor influencing castor oil quality is its packaging. Castor oil is susceptible to light and heat, which can cause it to degrade with time. High-quality castor oil is generally stored in dark amber or cobalt glass bottles to protect it from light and air.

Why It Matters: Light and heat can oxidize castor oil, reducing its potency and efficacy. Plastic bottles may potentially leak pollutants into the oil, particularly when exposed to sunshine or heat. Dark glass bottles provide superior protection and enhance the shelf life of the oil.

What to Look For: Choose castor oil stored in dark glass bottles to keep it powerful and effective for longer. Avoid clear plastic bottles, which might damage the oil and shorten its shelf life.

Consider the Source and Manufacturer Reputation

The manufacturer's reputation and methods have a significant impact on the quality of castor oil. Choosing a respected brand that is open about its sourcing and manufacturing techniques will help you guarantee that you are getting a high-quality product.

Why It Matters: Companies that promote sustainable sourcing, organic farming, and ethical manufacturing are more likely to create high-quality oils free of pollutants and chemicals. Reputable firms frequently use third-party testing to ensure the purity and quality of their products.

What to Look For: Choose brands that are open about their sourcing and production practices. Investigate the company's reputation, read customer reviews, and look for third-party tests or certifications that validate the oil's quality and purity.

Select the Right Castor Oil for Your Needs

As I said in the previous chapter, there are several varieties of castor oil available, each tailored to a certain requirement. Understanding the variations between these sorts can assist you in selecting the best product for your needs.

Cold-Pressed Castor Oil: This is the purest kind of castor oil, suitable for skincare, hair treatments, and internal use. It preserves all of the oil's inherent qualities and nutrients.

Jamaican Black Castor Oil: This variant involves burning the castor seeds before pressing the oil. The roasting procedure results in a dark hue and distinct aroma. Jamaican black castor oil is particularly popular for hair growth treatments because of its ability to stimulate circulation to the scalp, however it may not be ideal for sensitive skin types.

Refined Castor Oil: This oil has been treated to remove contaminants and odors. While refined castor oil may be appropriate for industrial use, it is frequently stripped of its essential components and is not suggested for skincare or internal usage.

What to Look for: Cold-pressed castor oil is best for overall health and beauty, especially if you have sensitive skin. Jamaican black castor oil is an excellent choice for people looking to promote hair growth. Avoid refined oils for personal care since they may not have the same healing powers as pure, unrefined oils.

Only use pharmaceutical-grade castor oil for internal or therapeutic uses. These oils have been specifically refined and verified for safety.

Finding high-quality castor oil is essential for really benefiting from its medicinal qualities. You can ensure that you are utilizing the best castor oil for your health, beauty, and wellness needs by purchasing cold-pressed, organic, and hexane-free goods, as well as paying attention to packaging, ingredients, and the manufacturer's reputation. Whether you use castor oil for skincare, hair development, or internal cures, purchasing a high-quality product will allow you to maximize its effectiveness while avoiding potentially dangerous additions or inferior alternatives.

What Professionals Say About Castor Oil

As the natural health movement grows, castor oil has received attention from professionals in holistic wellness, naturopathy, and natural therapies. Many experts in these fields recommend castor oil as a diverse and effective treatment for a variety of health and beauty issues. Castor oil has been praised by prominent experts for its unique ability to promote overall well-being, ranging from anti-inflammatory effects to detoxifying.

Holistic Health Experts on Castor Oil

Holistic health practitioners often emphasize the necessity of employing natural medicines that complement the body's natural healing mechanisms rather than upsetting them. Castor oil, with its plant-based origins and deep-penetrating characteristics, is an ideal fit for this philosophy, making it a popular ingredient in many holistic treatments.

Dr. David G. Williams, Natural Healer and Wellness Advocate.

Dr. David G. Williams[33], a well-known authority on alternative medicine, has long advocated for the use of castor oil in holistic health practices. He emphasizes the oil's importance in boosting the lymphatic system and facilitating cleansing.

"No drug exists that has the ability to improve lymphatic flow; however, the job can easily be handled through the topical application of castor oil."

---

33 (Williams, 1995)

Dr. Williams notes that applying castor oil packs to the belly stimulates lymphatic drainage and helps the body's natural cleansing process.

This insight highlights castor oil's unique ability to stimulate the lymphatic system, which is critical for immune function and overall health. Dr. Williams' recommendation of castor oil as a cleansing agent has prompted many holistic practitioners to include castor oil packs in treatments for liver health, immunological support, and inflammation control.

Dr. Joseph Mercola, Physician and Wellness Expert

Dr. Joseph Mercola34, a major advocate for natural medicine, also praises castor oil's therapeutic properties. He underlines its potent anti-inflammatory and antibacterial characteristics, which make it useful for a number of skin diseases, as well as its ability to promote hair growth.

"Castor oil is a great natural remedy for skin problems like acne, psoriasis, and eczema. It also works well to thicken and regrow hair, particularly when used as a scalp treatment."

Dr. Mercola notes that the ricinoleic acid in castor oil has powerful therapeutic effects that can be utilized to calm sensitive skin and increase hair follicle growth.

Dr. Mercola believes that by combining castor oil with essential oils such as peppermint or rosemary, people can increase its effectiveness in improving hair health and curing scalp issues.

---

34 (Mercola, 2016)

Naturopaths and Castor Oil

Castor oil is commonly used in the professions of naturopathic doctors (NDs) due to its numerous medicinal applications. Naturopaths praise the oil's capacity to handle both acute and chronic illnesses without the negative effects of medicines, such as enhancing digestive health and alleviating joint pain.

Dr. Edward Group: Naturopath, Natural Health Advocate.

Dr. Edward Group[35], a naturopath and the creator of Global Healing, is another supporter of castor oil, citing its role in supporting digestive health and its usage in castor oil packs to alleviate inflammation.

"Castor oil packs can help to relieve constipation, reduce inflammation, and support liver detoxification. It's one of the most effective natural remedies for improving digestive health."

Dr. Group emphasizes castor oil's ability to stimulate bowel movements and relieve digestive discomfort, as well as its efficacy in enhancing liver health through detoxification.

For patients suffering from constipation or other digestive difficulties, Dr. Group advises castor oil packs as a gentle yet effective alternative to harsh medication laxatives. He further mentions that using castor oil packs on a regular basis can help reduce chronic inflammation, which is frequently associated with digestive disorders such as IBS.

---

35 (Group, 2014)

Dr. Josh Axe, Naturopath and Functional Medicine Expert.

Dr. Josh Axe36, a naturopath and functional medicine expert, frequently recommends castor oil as part of a comprehensive treatment plan for joint pain, arthritis, and inflammation.

"Castor oil is an excellent natural treatment for joint pain and arthritis. Its anti-inflammatory properties can help reduce swelling and alleviate discomfort, particularly when used in conjunction with heat therapy."

Dr. Axe advises castor oil packs or massages for anyone suffering from inflammatory joint disorders since the oil penetrates deeply into the tissues and provides comfort.

In addition to its anti-inflammatory properties, Dr. Axe emphasizes castor oil's capacity to promote skin health by minimizing fine wrinkles, increasing skin suppleness, and healing skin irritations. According to him, castor oil's adaptability makes it an essential component of any natural medicine toolkit.

Herbalists on Castor Oil.

Herbalists, who specialize in the use of plants and plant-derived compounds to promote health, frequently advocate castor oil for skin, hair, and internal health. Castor oil has a long history of use as a plant-based oil for healing, making it a herbal medicine staple.

Rosemary Gladstar, a herbalist and author.

---

36 (Axe, 2018)

Rosemary Gladstar[37], one of the most famous herbalists in the United States, praises castor oil for its capacity to treat skin issues and promote healthy hair. In her publications, she frequently describes how to include castor oil into DIY skincare and haircare products.

"Castor oil has long been used for promoting healthy hair and treating dry, irritated skin. It's particularly effective in healing cracked hands and feet, and its thick, nourishing texture makes it ideal for deep moisturizing treatments."

Gladstar's promotion of castor oil's healing and moisturizing characteristics has impacted many people who choose herbal and natural skincare and haircare products. Her recipes frequently use castor oil as a crucial ingredient to cure everything from dandruff to eczema.

---

37 (Gladstar, 2012)

Success Stories

One of the most compelling reasons to investigate natural therapies such as castor oil is the success stories of people who have seen significant improvements in their health and beauty routines.

Castor oil's versatility, which includes enhanced skin texture and hair development as well as relief from chronic pain and digestive disorders, has gained it a dedicated following.

I have already shared my personal experience at the beginning of this book, and in this chapter, I want offer you real-life testimonials from other people who have included castor oil into their everyday lives, demonstrating how this humble oil has significantly improved their health.

While each story is unique, they share a similar thread: castor oil's capacity to naturally and successfully manage a wide range of health conditions.

The Path to Radiant Skin for Patricia

Patricia Johnson, a 60-year-old retired teacher, had dry, sensitive skin her entire life. Her skin became less elastic as she grew older, and the small creases around her mouth and eyes became more noticeable. Patricia says, *"I tried everything—prescription treatments, high-end moisturizers, and serums—but nothing seemed to give me the long-lasting hydration my skin so desperately needed."*

Patricia made the decision to test castor oil one day after reading about its advantages for aged skin. She began adding a basic castor oil treatment to her nightly skincare routine. Patricia says,

"Every night before bed, I mixed a few drops of castor oil with rosehip oil and applied it to my face." "I saw a noticeable change in just a few weeks. My skin appeared more moisturized, plumper, and had fewer visible fine wrinkles.

Patricia started using castor oil as a go-to remedy for keeping her skin looking young, going beyond just a moisturizer. *"I adore the way my skin seems now. It feels healthier overall and is softer and more vibrant. I regret not learning about castor oil sooner!*

Sarah's Transition to Thick Locks from Thinning Hair

Sarah Thompson, a busy working mother in her late 40s, battled hair thinning for a long time. Her hair was scant and fragile from years of style, stress, and hormonal swings. *"I felt so self-conscious about my hair, and I was always trying to hide the thinning areas,"* Sarah says. *"I tried a lot of pricey hair treatments, but nothing seemed to work."*

Castor oil was suggested by a friend, and that was Sarah's turning point. She admits, *"At first, I was skeptical, but I was willing to try anything."* In order to improve circulation, Sarah started applying castor oil to her scalp twice a week and combining it with a few drops of essential rosemary oil. *"I would rinse it out after a few hours of leaving it on."* I was astounded by the outcomes after a few months—my hair felt healthier and thicker. In places that had been thinning for years, I spotted fresh growth.

Sarah is still using castor oil now and is very happy with her hair care regimen. *"My self-assurance has returned. My hair seems to be stronger and more resilient than it has ever been."*

Margaret's Joint Pain Relief

Margaret Davis, a 65-year-old retired accountant, had suffered from persistent arthritis in her knees for more than ten years. She frequently found it difficult to move about freely due to the pain, and she had trouble finding respite. *"I didn't want to constantly depend on painkillers,"* Margaret declares. *"I was searching for a natural remedy that would not have any negative side effects to help with the pain."*

Margaret made the decision to try castor oil after learning about its anti-inflammatory properties in literature. She started massaging her knees with castor oil packs every night. *"I used a heating pad for about 45 minutes every night, and I wrapped a cloth around my knees that had been soaked in warm castor oil,"* she says. It was calming, and after a few weeks, I noticed a noticeable change. The discomfort and stiffness were considerably easier to handle.

Margaret now uses castor oil as part of her regular pain regimen. Although it's not a cure, it's significantly improved my quality of life. I feel more energetic than I have in years, and I can walk more comfortably.

Digestive Relief with Diane

Diane Miller, a 58-year-old retired woman, has spent years battling intestinal problems. She had been experiencing chronic constipation and bloating on a daily basis, and she had attempted numerous therapies without much luck. Diane remembers, *"It was frustrating and really affected my mood and energy levels."*

Diane happened to find castor oil listed as a possible cure for stomach problems one day while looking through natural health cures. The concept of utilizing a natural oil to treat constipation piqued her interest, she adds. Diane started taking a tablespoon of castor oil internally as needed to encourage regular bowel movements and started using it as a mild laxative. It was a complete success! I would experience relief in a matter of hours, and this laxative wasn't as harsh as the others I'd tried.

Additionally, Diane began applying castor oil packs to her stomach to help with digestion and relieve bloating. *"For me, it's changed the game. Now that my digestion has greatly improved, I feel more in charge of my health."*

Linda's Success Story with Hair Growth

The 64-year-old grandma Linda Carson has always loved having long, thick hair. However, her hair grew brittle and thinner with time. She says, *"Seeing my hair lose its shine and volume was heartbreaking."* She made the decision to alter her hairstyle after learning about the advantages of castor oil.

Twice a week, Linda started massaging her scalp with a mixture of castor oil and peppermint essential oil. She explains, *"I'd massage it in and leave it overnight." "I didn't notice much at first, but after a few months, my hair felt so much healthier and started to grow thicker."*

Linda is now sticking to this easy regimen, and her hair has never looked better. *"I'm so glad I tried castor oil." "It's a crucial component of my beauty regimen now, and I can't fathom doing without it."*

These stories demonstrate the power of castor oil for a variety of health and cosmetic issues. Whether it is used to support healthy skin, encourage hair development, ease joint pain, or improve digestion, castor oil has gained widespread acceptance as a reliable natural medicine.

Final Thoughts

As we near the end of our journey into the fascinating world of castor oil, it is evident that this simple oil is anything but ordinary. What started as a natural medicine with ancient roots has grown into a diverse, scientifically validated therapy for a variety of health, beauty, and wellbeing issues. Whether you want to rejuvenate your skin, nurture your hair, aid digestion, or detoxify your body, castor oil is a natural, effective way to improve your health.

Throughout the book, we have seen how flexible castor oil is. Castor oil has a wide range of applications. It has the potential to nourish and protect the body, whether used externally or internally.

One of the most important insights from this experience is the value of using high-quality castor oil. I've talked about how cold-pressed, organic, and hexane-free castor oil preserves its natural healing characteristics, making it the ideal choice for health and beauty treatments. Understanding the distinction between high- and low-quality goods allows you to make more informed selections and reap the full advantages of this Incredible product.

The genuine beauty of castor oil comes from its simplicity. With just one bottle of oil, you may make a variety of treatments to replace chemical-laden household items. The recipes I've published, which combine castor oil with essential oils, give you practical options to develop bespoke therapies for your specific requirements.

Castor oil is a long-term, effective, and environmentally responsible option that fits smoothly into your lifestyle. What distinguishes it from other products is not just its ability to treat specific illnesses, but also its potential to promote general wellness. It promotes a holistic approach, which works in tandem with your body's natural processes to repair, renew, and balance. This is consistent with a broader attitude of self-care, which prioritizes natural, gentle remedies over hasty cures or harsh treatments. Castor oil is a reminder that nature frequently supplies the best tools for maintaining health and beauty, and that simplicity and constancy can yield significant effects.

If there's one takeaway from this book, it's that castor oil is a versatile, economical, and easily available tool for improving your health and wellbeing. The goal is to incorporate it into your daily self-care regimen and experiment with it to fully realize its possibilities. Whether you're drawn to castor oil for its skincare advantages, digestive assistance, or ability to relieve chronic pain, it's a natural gift that can help you take control of your health in a natural, lasting way.

Consider this book a guide, but be aware that your journey with castor oil does not end here. The more you utilize it, the more benefits you'll notice.
As you go, continue to study, experiment, and tailor your routines to your body's specific needs.

Castor oil has endured the test of time because it works!

Your Journey with Castor Oil

As you've discovered throughout this book, castor oil is more than a simple therapy; it's a gateway to natural, long-term health and beauty solutions. Castor oil's flexibility makes it a valuable companion in your wellness research, from encouraging bright skin and stronger hair to aiding digestion and alleviating pain. Now it's time for you to take the first step and start your own castor oil journey.

The thoughts and tips you've learned here are only the beginning. What really counts is how you choose to use them in your own life, how you personalize castor oil's many advantages to your own requirements, and how you include it into your self-care regimen. Every person's journey is unique, and castor oil's adaptability allows it to fit seamlessly into your daily routine.

Why Documenting Your Journey is Important

One of the most rewarding parts of natural wellness is witnessing the progression over time. Whether you're taking castor oil to improve your look, develop thicker hair, or treat chronic pain, keeping track of your progress can provide you with a sense of success and perspective. Tracking your experiences allows you to identify tiny improvements that would otherwise go unreported. It also teaches you what works best for your body and when you might need to make changes.

By documenting your journey, you will not only improve your affinity with castor oil but also encourage others to investigate its benefits. Your personal success stories— whether they involve clearer skin, better digestion, or healthier hair—may inspire others to adopt a more natural approach to their health.

Start Your Journey Today

As you begin your journey, keep in mind that consistency is paramount. Small, consistent actions will produce the best benefits, whether you incorporate castor oil into your nightly skincare routine, use it as a weekly hair mask, or use it for pain relief as needed. With patience and persistence, you'll begin to see the benefits that castor oil provides.

To begin started, try concentrating on one aspect of your wellness that you would like to enhance. Is it brighter skin, stronger hair, or improved digestion? Begin with a simple castor oil application that meets your needs, and progress from there. The road does not have to be overwhelming; start with a single step and let the advantages unfold organically over time.

Your Wellness Journey Begins Now

Castor oil is a natural gift that has been loved for ages, and now it's your turn to take advantage of its benefits. This book has given you the information and resources you need to get started; now it is up to you to take the next step. The route to natural health and beauty is full of discoveries, and with castor oil by your side, you'll be ready to embrace a healthier, more radiant lifestyle.

Your journey is only beginning, and each small step you take with castor oil contributes to a more balanced, natural approach to wellness. Remember that you are not alone

So, take the initial step, accept the possibilities, and allow castor oil guide you to a higher level of well-being.

Appendix 1: List of all the individual components used across the recipes

Oils and Butters:

- Castor oil
- Shea butter
- Coconut oil
- Grapeseed oil
- Almond oil
- Jojoba oil
- Argan oil
- Olive oil
- Rosehip oil
- Black seed oil
- Comfrey oil
- Arnica oil
- Evening primrose oil
- Calendula oil
- Turmeric oil

Essential Oils:

- Peppermint essential oil
- Lavender essential oil
- Eucalyptus essential oil
- Tea tree essential oil
- Frankincense essential oil
- Chamomile essential oil
- Rosemary essential oil
- Ginger essential oil
- Cypress essential oil
- Thyme essential oil
- Camphor essential oil
- Myrrh essential oil
- Lemon essential oil
- Oregano essential oil
- Clove essential oil
- Rose essential oil

Other Ingredients:

- Honey
- Aloe vera gel
- Witch hazel
- Baking soda
- Apple cider vinegar
- Lemon juice

Bibliography

Axe, J. (2018). *Using Castor Oil to Treat Joint Pain Naturally.* Retrieved from Dr. Axe Functional Medicine Blog: draxe.com

Broglie, K. &. (2015). Evaluation of castor oil as a pest repellent in integrated pest management. *Journal of Pest Science,,* 88(4), 679-688.

Ghadiri, M. G. (2012). The role of castor oil in the treatment of hypothyroidism: A case study. . *Journal of Herbal Medicine, ,* 6(3), 210-214.

Gladstar, R. (2012). Herbal Healing for Women: Treating Common Health Issues with Herbs. . *Healing Arts Press,,* 152-155.

Goto, E. S.-2. (2002). *Low-concentration homogenized castor oil eye drops for noninflamed obstructive meibomian gland dysfunction.* Retrieved from https://doi.org/10.1016/s0161-6420(02)01262-9

Group, E. (2014). *Castor Oil Packs for Digestive Health.* Retrieved from Global Healing Blog,: globalhealing.com

Kazemzadeh, R. H. (2017). Effects of castor oil packs on primary dysmenorrhea: A pilot study. *Iranian Journal of Nursing and Midwifery Research,* 22(3), 251-256.

McGarey, D. &. (2001). Castor oil packs in the treatment of musculoskeletal injuries. . *Alternative Therapies in Health and Medicine,* 7(5), 97-101.

McGarey, M. (1993). The effects of castor oil packs on the lymphatic system and detoxification processes. . *ournal of Naturopathic Medicine,* 4(2), 44-48.

Mercola, J. (2016). The Benefits of Castor Oil for Hair and Skin. . *Mercola Natural Health Newsletter,* 8(12), 24-29.

Muller-Lissner, S. (2010). Effect of stimulant laxatives on gastrointestinal function. *The American Journal of Gastroenterology,* 105(3), 743-750.

O'Dell, K. D. (2018). Fatty acid-based lubricants: Green solutions for sustainable future applications. *Green Chemistry,,* 20(12), 2675-2684.

Palmer, B. (2014). Managing hyperkalemia caused by medications that promote potassium retention and diuretics. . *The Journal of Clinical Hypertension, ,* 16(7), 546-552.

Patel, M. G. (2016). Biodiesel production from castor oil: Challenges and prospects. . *Renewable and Sustainable Energy Reviews,* 65, 793-810.

Petersen, B. &. (2014). Phototoxicity of essential oils: UV-induced erythema and pigmentation caused by topical bergamot oil. *Photodermatology, Photoimmunology & Photomedicine,* 30(2), 107-113.

Pliny the Elder, T. N. (Plin. Nat. 23.41). *http://data.perseus.org/citations/urn:cts:latinLit:phi0978.phi0 01.perseus-eng1:23.41.* Retrieved from http://data.perseus.org/citations/urn:cts:latinLit:phi097 8.phi001.perseus-eng1:23.41

Sevastre, B. N. (2001). The anti-inflammatory and anti-nociceptive effects of castor oil on experimental models. *Phytotherapy Research,* 25(4), 664-670.

Sevastre, B. N. (2011). Castor oil's effects on sun-damaged skin and its potential for reducing hyperpigmentation. *Phytotherapy Research,,* 25(4), 664-670.

Sevastre, B. N. (2011). Castor oil's role in conditioning hair and reducing breakage. *Phytotherapy Research,* 25(4), 664-670.

Sevastre, B. N. (2011). The anti-inflammatory and anti-nociceptive effects of castor oil on experimental models. . *Phytotherapy Research,* 25(4), 664-670.

Sevastre, B. N. (2011). The anti-inflammatory and skin-soothing properties of castor oil for treating skin conditions. *Phytotherapy Research,* 25(4), 664-670.

Suttie, J. (2009). Vitamin K and human nutrition. *Blood Journal, ,* 93(6), 1422-1430.

Swenson, P. S. (1990). Antimicrobial effects of ricinoleic acid in the treatment of dandruff. *Journal of Applied Microbiology,* 69(1), 111-115.

Swenson, P. S. (1990). The anti-inflammatory activity of ricinoleic acid and its influence on gut health. *Journal of Applied Microbiology,* 69(1), 111-115.

Swenson, P. S. (1990). The antimicrobial activity of castor oil and its relation to ricinoleic acid content. . *Journal of Applied Microbiology,* 69(1), 111-115.

Swenson, P. S. (1990). The antimicrobial activity of castor oil and its relation to ricinoleic acid content. . *Journal of Applied Microbiology, ,* 69(1), 111-115.

Tournier, C. M. (2006). Effectiveness of castor oil as a stimulant laxative in the treatment of constipation. *Journal of Clinical Gastroenterology,,* 40(6), 473-477.

Venzke, L. C. (2008). The efficacy of castor oil in relieving menopausal symptoms. . *Menopause Journal,* 15(4), 685-692.

Verallo-Rowell, V. D.-T. (2008). Castor oil as a hydrating agent for sensitive skin types. *International Journal of Trichology,* 59(3), 341-352.

Verallo-Rowell, V. D.-T. (2008). Novel antibacterial and emollient effects of coconut and castor oil on human skin. . *The Journal of Cosmetic Science,* 59(3), 341-352.

Verallo-Rowell, V. D.-T. (2008). Novel emollient and skin-firming effects of castor oil on aging skin. *The Journal of Cosmetic Science,,* 59(3), 341-352.

Verallo-Rowell, V. D.-T. (2008). The role of castor oil in stimulating hair growth and improving scalp health. *International Journal of Trichology,,* 59(3), 341-352.

Vieira, C. E. (2000). The anti-inflammatory properties of ricinoleic acid in managing skin conditions. *Journal of Investigative Dermatology,,* 293(2), 745-751.

Vieira, C. E. (2002). Ricinoleic acid, a specific agonist of capsaicin receptor, induces hyperalgesia in guinea-pigs. *Journal of Pharmacology and Experimental Therapeutics,,* 293(2), 745-751.

Vieira, C. E. (2002). Ricinoleic acid, a specific agonist of capsaicin receptor, induces hyperalgesia in guinea-pigs. Journal of Pharmacology and Experimental Therapeutics, .

wenson, P. S. (1990). The moisturizing and anti-aging effects of ricinoleic acid-rich castor oil. *Journal of Applied Microbiology,,* 69(1), 111-115.

Williams, D. (1995). Improving Lymphatic Flow with Castor Oil Packs. *Alternative Medicine Digest,* 5, 72-79.

Video Tutorials

In this section, we've included a series of supplementary videos with Barbara O'Neill herself, who shows how to make various castor oil remedies. From beginning to end, you will be guided through the processes and practices, allowing you to follow along with confidence. Simply scan the QR code and you'll be led directly to the videos for hands-on learning. These instructions are intended to make the procedure simple to understand and implement in your own house.

How to make Castor oil Compress

Helps for joint pain and arthritis

Improve bone spurs and kidney stones

Additionally, visit my website www.gymeaverse.com **to discover more tips, tricks, and explore my other books on holistic wellness and herbal remedies.**